How to Do Your Own
DIVORCE
in Texas

Ed Sherman, Attorney

Eighth Edition

Nolo Press Occidental
2425 Porter Street, Suite 19, Soquel, CA 95073
831 479-1520

Printing History

Nolo Press is committed to keeping its books up to date. Each new printing is revised to include any recent changes in the law. When the changes are extensive or drastic in some way, the book is printed as a new edition. This book was updated and printed on the last date listed below:

First edition	August 1980	**Fifth edition**	January 1994
Second printing	August 1983	Second printing	January 1995
Third printing	August 1985	**Sixth edition**	January 1996
Second edition	June 1986	Second printing	April 1997
Second printing	June 1987	**Seventh edition**	January 1998
Third printing	June 1988	Second printing	March 1999
Third edition	January 1990	Third printing	October 1999
Second printing	April 1990	Fourth printing	August 2000
Fourth edition	October 1991	**Eighth edition**	October 2001
Second printing	March 1993		

ISBN: 0-944508-38-3

Library of Congress Catalog Number: 2001091839

This book is dedicated to all of my clients
and to my ex-wife
from whom I have learned so much
about the subject in these pages

Design and graphics: Ed Sherman
Typography: Stephen Pollard

Contents

Part One: All About Divorce

Contents

Part Two: How to Do Your Own Divorce

Part One

All About Divorce

A. Some Basic Information About Divorce

1. What Is a Divorce?

How many of these statements do you feel are true?

A divorce

a) is a legal dissolution of the bonds of matrimony.

b) is filing two or three forms and getting a judge to sign the last one.

c) means a lot of decisions have to be made and some loose ends tied up.

d) is not a weapon to use against your spouse.

e) is legally/emotionally desirable only when it is really all over and finished for your marriage, with no doubts and no hope or desire for putting it back together.

f) should not be done when in a highly emotional state. You have important decisions that should be made clearly, and it rarely hurts legally if you wait.

g) is a lot better when it's over than when you are thinking it over or doing it.

h) You can do yourself a whole lot of good by reading this book to find out:

- the rules of divorce.
- practical decisions which must be made.
- information to help make them.
- step-by-step instructions showing exactly how a divorce is done, with forms to do it.
- where to get help if you need it.

(Answers on next page.)

Answers: True. All true.

2. Can You Do Your Own Divorce?

Yes!

If you can read and understand this book, and if you can follow the clear and easy instructions in it, then you can do your own divorce. Over 500,000 people in Texas have used our book to do their own divorces without an attorney, so you can probably do it too.

No!

There are a few cases where you can not do your own divorce without help. You can not do your own divorce:

a) if your spouse hires an attorney to file legal papers to oppose you.

b) if your spouse successfully avoids service of the legal papers (see section 9).

c) if your spouse is on *active* military duty and will *not* sign a waiver form.

d) if the custody of a minor child of your marriage has ever come before a Texas court.

e) if you need an award for alimony and can't get your spouse to agree to it in a marital settlement agreement you *may* need a lawyer.

f) if you read this book and still have doubts, questions, or trouble making decisions.

Even if you feel that you cannot do your own divorce, you should still read this book because it will tell you how to get the best and most economical legal help, and it will also tell you all about your divorce case — things many attorneys do not take the time to explain.

Please do *not* rush into doing your own divorce while caught up in emotional pressures or in desperation. You have many decisions to make, and they should be made calmly and clearly.

If your case does not come under any of the exceptions listed above, then you can almost certainly do your own divorce. Read on!

3. Advantages to Being Your Own Attorney

a. It's much cheaper to do it yourself

Perhaps the most obvious advantage to doing your own divorce is the savings in cost. Most attorneys collect a fairly stiff fee for doing even a simple uncontested divorce. They average about $500 for doing a job that is quite simple and that is usually done by an underpaid secretary anyway. In all fairness, it must be said that some urban areas of Texas have price competition among attorneys, who advertise their low prices for simple uncontested divorce cases. If you happen to live in one of those areas, you may be able to find someone to do your case for as little as $100, plus court costs.

A divorce for $100 is a pretty good deal, but you can expect to get what you pay for in this as in everything else. Even at full price, lawyers tend not to give you much time or information, and this is especially true in the cut-rate law office. Rarely, if ever, do you get to speak with the lawyer, and then only briefly. It's hard to get personal advice and attention, and you probably won't be able to get the lawyer on the phone very easily. You almost always end up wondering what's going on, but there's no one to talk to about it.

Not all cut-rate lawyers operate this way. There are always those few overworked and underpaid souls who are dedicated to counseling, education, and an ethical practice. More about them later, and more about how to look for an attorney when you need one (see section 12). The point here is that you save *at least* $100 to $500 by doing it yourself.

b. Keeping it simple

A lot of people start off with simple cases that don't necessarily end up that way. Lawyers have a way of making almost anything more complicated. This is because of the way they are trained, the way they operate, and the way they think. A lawyer is a combatant. Our system of justice is known as "the adversary system," and it is literally and historically rooted in the medieval field of honor where trial by combat meant that whoever survived was right.

Law schools have no course requirement in counseling or communications skills, and very few lawyers voluntarily acquire any. Rather, they are strongly trained in aggressive and defensive paperwork, and how to get the most financial advantage in every case. Is this the attitude you want in your divorce?

Most divorces are fairly sensitive and it doesn't take much to stir them up. Your average attorney is just too likely to make things worse instead of better. Here's just one very common example. Let's say that a couple is separated and has things sort of stable. It's a situation where lots of sleeping dogs are being left to lie. Then one spouse goes to an attorney to start the divorce. Pretty soon the lawyer files a Petition asking for more property and support than can reasonably be expected. That's a standard lawyer procedure — lawyers believe it is their duty to get the best deal they can for their client, and they think it pays to ask for a lot so they can bargain their way back down. When the other spouse gets a copy of the Petition, it's a big shock and they think they have been deceived. There's tension and there's trouble, not to mention mistrust and hurt. There's also probably going to be another attorney in the case, since the upset spouse wants to get a different kind of advice than the other side is giving.

Two attorneys start off costing just double, but pretty soon they start writing letters and filing motions and doing standard attorney-type things, just like they were taught. Now we have a contested case, more fees and charges, and a couple of very upset spouses. Sure hope they don't have kids. The fees in contested cases can run from *a lot* all the way up to *everything*.

This is just one example to represent many others, but they all lead to the same conclusion: if you do it yourself, there's a much better chance of keeping a simple case easy and simple.

c. Personal satisfaction

It's a bit more trouble if you do it yourself, but this way you will understand every step. You are completely in charge of your own case, your own decisions, and your own life. It feels good to stand on your own two feet.

This book is not designed to replace an attorney, it is meant to help you decide whether or not you *need* one. The law says that you have the right to have an attorney represent you if you want one. No law says that you *must* have one.

The time once was when people did most things for themselves. Not so today, when there's an expert for everything. The lawyer is one of those experts you're not ever supposed to do without. The lawyer is an expert on words whose special talent is knowing what to say, who to say it to, and when to say it. If, after you read this book, you know what to say, who to say it to, and when to say it, then you won't need a lawyer. The lawyer has special knowledge and special experience to help you make decisions. If, after reading this book, you can make your own decisions, you won't need a lawyer.

4. Making Decisions

Part of the service you are supposed to get from a lawyer is help with making decisions about your affairs. They know which things have to be decided and they know the general standards and rules by which things are done in the courts. This is what the first part of this book is all about. It tells you what needs doing and the way things are generally done in cases where there is no fight. It gives you information and help with making your own decisions.

If, after reading this book, you can make your own decisions based on your own knowledge, then you probably do not need a lawyer. If you read this book and still have doubts or questions, then you probably should have professional advice. It may be that you can find an attorney who will help you settle your mind, then you can go on to do the rest on your own. Section 12 tells you how to find such a person.

Things That Must Be Decided

- that the marriage should be ended forever, and

- how to divide any property and bills that you may have accumulated during the marriage.

Where there are no minor children, that's all there is to it. Where there are children, you must also decide:

- who is to have custody of the children,

- how visitation is to be arranged, and

- how much is to be paid for support.

As far as the law is concerned, this is what a divorce is all about — settling the practical affairs of the couple and watching out for the well-being of the children. These are the things you must decide about in order to get a divorce. If your spouse is in the picture and cares about what happens in the divorce, then either you must be able to talk things over and agree on these things, or you must be sure that your spouse will not get a lawyer and oppose you legally.

5. Agreed Divorce and Default Divorce

When a divorce lawsuit is filed, it raises the issues outlined above. These issues can be resolved in one of only three ways:

- by agreement of the parties,

- by default, or

- by contest.

In the *agreed case*, the parties get together and settle the issues before anyone goes to court. In the *default case*, the Respondent is properly notified of the divorce lawsuit, but does nothing about it, and no Answer is filed within the permitted time. A person who does not show up for a contest loses by default. In the *contested case*, the Respondent files an Answer and comes into court to do legal battle before a judge, who makes a decision in the case. You cannot do your own divorce if an Answer is filed.

a. The default divorce

This kind of case is easy to do, assuming you can get papers served on your spouse. After service, and after the waiting periods, you go in for a hearing and get your divorce Decree. Even if your spouse barks, there is no bite so long as no Answer is filed.

b. The agreed divorce

If your spouse is in the picture and cares about what happens, then you must make efforts to reach an agreement on the legal issues of your divorce. Look what you gain by having an agreement before you go through with your divorce:

a) It is cheaper and easier. You save $50.00 or more on filing and service fees, and you have less work and fewer details to take care of.

b) It is more certain as to how things will be ordered at the hearing. The judge will be very likely to follow the terms of any agreement that is not obviously unfair.

c) It will help the Respondent feel better about letting the divorce go through without contest or representation, since the terms of the divorce Decree are pretty much settled ahead of time.

d) The divorce is much easier to do, both in preparing the paperwork and at the hearing.

e) It feels better. It invariably leads to better relations with your ex-spouse. Where there are children, this is especially important and worth a great deal.

The agreed divorce has so many advantages that if there is any chance at all of working things out with your spouse, you should work for it. If things do not work out, you can always serve papers later and proceed as a default case.

Some truly lucky people are able to get a lot of cooperation from their spouses. These are the mature folks who can take care of business and keep any personal problems separate, where they belong. These kinds of cases are almost certain to be easy and relatively pleasant to do, and they create the foundation for a very successful divorce.

c. To fight, or not to fight — is that the question?

This is the point that divides the easy cases from the hard ones. The main reason for a difficult time with divorce is that the couple either wants to fight, or just can't keep from it. These people are angry or hurt and want to hurt back, to make things hard. They want to use the law as a weapon to force their spouse into some sort of response. The law rarely has this result; rather it almost always turns a contested divorce into a very unpleasant and very expensive failure. Oh yes, the divorce will go through, but no one is ever happy about it. No one really wins a court battle. If your case is in any danger of becoming one of these, remember this: it is one thing to get an order against someone, but it is very much another thing to enforce that order. Especially in cases where there are children, a divorce is not a final solution, since you have to deal with each other in the future because of the kids. In more ways than one, it really pays to work things out.

d. Working things out

If you can't agree about basic things peacefully, maybe let some time pass. Wait to see if things settle down. Maybe get a copy of our *Practical Divorce Solutions* for techniques to resolve conflicts and settle disagreements with your spouse (see order form in back of this book).

It may be very helpful to get a copy of this book, send it to your spouse, and then try to discuss various sections in it. This is a good idea because your spouse may misunderstand what a divorce is about, and informed people are usually less emotional and irrational. It can get you talking about practical, constructive things. Also, the book helps to make these points:

a) Fighting will not prevent the divorce, it will only make it more unpleasant and much more expensive.

b) Even contested divorces are decided according to the standards discussed in this book. Any monetary advantage gained by a fight is often wiped out by the fees and costs of the battle. How do you value the emotional strain and future relations with your spouse and children?

If the reason you can't agree is emotional, or basic inability to communicate, you can still be very successful if you can both agree to involve a third person. A trusted friend, a member of the clergy, or a professional mediator or counselor can often be very helpful at getting things worked out. It's worth a try.

Do not try to proceed with your own divorce if you and your spouse are in such active and antagonistic opposition that your spouse is likely to get an attorney to fight you in court.

If you are not certain what your spouse's attitude and response will be, whether your spouse will really oppose you (or is just bluffing?), then you might consider going ahead with doing your own divorce. See what happens when your spouse is confronted with the reality of a court action. If your spouse gets an attorney to file response papers, then you must be ready to get one too. Always cover your bets.

6. Grounds for Divorce

In order to get a divorce, you have to show a court that you have a legally approved reason, known as "grounds," for your divorce.

Before 1970, in order to get a divorce you had to show that your spouse was bad or wrong — somehow at fault. This attitude definitely did not help anyone, and generally tended to make too many cases harder. Finally, the Texas legislature created a "no fault" form of divorce by providing legal grounds for dissolving a marriage without anyone having to be accused of anything. But they did it with language that would choke a horse or make an ordinary person snicker, and now we must slavishly use and say these words like a magical spell. It sometimes helps to look at it that way.

The grounds of insupportability: You can be divorced if your marriage "... has become insupportable because of discord or conflict of personalities that destroys the legitimate ends of the marriage relationship and prevents any reasonable expectation of reconciliation." This probably means that you don't get along in a way that seems both important and permanent. But you can't just say it this way, that would be too easy. Instead, when you go into court you must tell the judge exactly those words quoted above. If you had an attorney he or she would say the words for you, then ask you, "Isn't that true?" while nodding "Yes." You would then say "Yes," and that would be that. If you can bear the burden of saying these words on your own, then you don't need the attorney. It is, by the way, almost unheard of for a divorce not to be granted because of insufficient grounds.

There are six other grounds for divorce, two of which also involve no fault (living apart for more than three years and confinement in a mental hospital), and four of which involve fault (cruelty, adultery, conviction of a felony, and abandonment). Way over 99% of all cases are run on the grounds of "insupportability." Even if your case falls under one of the other categories, you still call it "insupportability." It's easier and it's the expected thing. That's all this book shows you how to do. In fact, you would stick out like a sore thumb if you tried anything else.

7. Jurisdiction (Power of the Court)

"Jurisdiction" means the legal right and power to make and enforce orders. In a divorce case, you are asking the court to make orders about your marriage, your property, your kids, and your spouse. The court has power to make orders about matters within the borders of Texas, so if you, your spouse, the kids, and the property are all in Texas, everything is fine. Just show that you satisfy the residency requirement, and you're on your way. But where would a Texas judge get off making orders about a spouse or kids or property if they are in some other state?

If your spouse resides permanently outside of Texas, then the court cannot have personal jurisdiction over your spouse unless your case satisfies the requirements of the "long-arm jurisdiction" rules. As a matter of fact, in many cases, you can get along just fine without having personal jurisdiction over your spouse. This is where there are no children, no property outside of Texas that you want to have, and no need to order your spouse to pay debts. But where there is a child, or important property outside of Texas that you want, or a need to order your spouse to pay debts, then you cannot do your own divorce in Texas unless you satisfy the long-arm rules.

"Long-arm jurisdiction" is, just as it sounds, when the court gets the right to make orders that reach out beyond the borders of Texas. There are actually two long-arm rules — the "marital long-arm" and the "parent/child long-arm."

a) **The marital long-arm:** If your spouse permanently resides outside of Texas, then the court can have personal jurisdiction over your spouse only if Texas is the last state in which you and your spouse had marital cohabitation (lived together as man and wife) and if your divorce suit is started within two years of the last time you cohabited. Even if you cannot satisfy this rule, you can still do your divorce if you do not need an order for the transfer of out-of-state property or for the payment of debts.

b) **The parent/child long-arm:** If there is a child, then you must satisfy this rule. The court can have jurisdiction over your case only if:

    i) your spouse is personally served with Citation while in Texas; *or*

    ii) your spouse consents to jurisdiction in Texas, by appearing in court or filing a document such as the Waiver (See Chapter 6); *or*

    iii) the child resides in Texas because of some act of your spouse, or with your spouse's approval; *or*

    iv) your spouse resided in Texas and provided prenatal expenses or support for the child (this is presumed if you and your spouse were living together during the pregnancy); *or*

    v) the child was conceived in Texas.

There may be other ways for the court to get power to act in your case, but you will need an attorney to explore them, and to plead them to the court properly.

8. Residency Requirements

Residency in Texas is what gives the court power to dissolve your marriage. No matter where you were married, some other state or some other country, if you meet the residency requirement, you can be divorced in Texas.

The residency requirement: In the period immediately before filing your divorce, either you or your spouse must have been a domiciliary of Texas for at least six months and a resident of the county where you file it for at least 90 days.

You are a "domiciliary" of Texas if you have your residence here with the intention to live here permanently. It's a matter of your intentions as much as your presence. It is okay to be absent on a temporary trip so long as you always intend to return. A person does not lose his or her domicile if absent from the state for military or public service for the state or nation. You are a "resident" of a county when you live there, no matter what your intentions. Being temporarily absent for a short trip does not interrupt residency.

9. *Notice to Your Spouse*

A lawsuit, in our system, is regarded as a struggle between two contestants, conducted before an impartial authority (judge). The one who is most "right" wins. It seems obvious (doesn't it?) that you can't have a proper contest if the other side doesn't even know one is going on.

The court cannot act in your case unless you can properly notify your spouse of the lawsuit. Chapter 6 shows how this is done, but in general terms, either your spouse must sign a Waiver stating that court papers have been received, or else the papers must be served properly by a Sheriff. If your spouse is on active military duty, then the only way you can do your own divorce is if your spouse will sign the Waiver. If your spouse successfully avoids service, or if your spouse is on active military duty and refuses to sign a Waiver, you will need the help of an attorney to proceed with your case.

If your spouse is long gone and all your attempts to locate him/her have failed, you are in for a little more work and expense. The law still requires that the missing spouse be given proper notice, but says you can do that by publishing your Citation in a newspaper. If this is your situation, you can get forms and instructions for "Citation by Publication" or "Citation by Posting" by sending a check for $6.00 to Nolo Press. Use the order form in the back of this book.

Proper notice means, among other things, that your spouse gets a copy of your Petition, and so can be presumed to know what the suit is about and more or less what you want. After proper notice, a lawsuit can go one of three ways:

- by agreement,
- by default, *or*
- by contest.

The best and easiest way is if you work it out by agreement, of course. The hardest way is where your spouse gets an attorney and files an Answer on time and you end up in a legal battle. The most common way is by default.

10. Waiting Periods

a. Waiting period before the hearing

The hearing is the time when you get your divorce, but you cannot rush right into it. After filing your Petition, you must wait at least 60 days before you have your hearing. Because of the way the law is worded, the 60-day period can sometimes be tricky to compute, so many lawyers consider it good practice to play it safe by waiting two months and two weeks. If your spouse signs a Waiver, this is the only waiting period that must be satisfied before the hearing.

If your spouse was "served," there are three different waiting periods, all of which must be satisfied. You must not have your hearing sooner than:

1) two months plus two weeks from the date you filed your Petition, *and*

2) 27 days from the date your spouse was served, *and*

3) 12 days from the date the Officer's Return (on the Citation) is filed with the District Clerk (See Chapter 6).

Please note that these times include a safety margin to cover possible problems with computing time "legally."

b. Waiting to remarry

You are not free to marry anyone else (except the person you just divorced) for 30 days after the judge orders your divorce.

11. Change of Name

In a divorce case, if it is requested by either party, the judge will change the name of either spouse. In actual practice, this rule is almost always used to restore a former name to the wife, but the way the law reads, you can change the name of either spouse to any name they used before. The court *must* grant your name change request unless they state in the Decree a reason for denying the change. They may no longer deny a change of name just to keep the last names of the parents and children the same.

12. How to Find the Right Attorney

If you need an attorney, one of your biggest problems is going to be to find the right one. Not just any old lawyer will do. You've got to shop around.

If you have trouble with some part of doing your own divorce, or if you and your spouse are trying to work out terms and get stuck, or if you need more information or legal advice, or for any reason at all, you may decide that a little time spent in conference with an attorney would be worthwhile. Instead of having an attorney do the whole job, you might have him or her help you with just part of it. Some attorneys may not be willing to do this. You have to shop around.

Shopping for an attorney is very much like shopping for melons. You not only have to check the prices, but you also have to see if they "feel" right to you. You have the right to ask questions, look things over, and be choosy about whom you hire to take on such a major personal role in your life.

The best way to find an attorney is through some friend or trusted person who has had a satisfactory personal experience with one. But don't forget to check things out for yourself. Don't be intimidated. Call around on the telephone to find out how much an initial interview will cost, and how much the whole case might cost. See if you like the way the attorney and the law office staff treat you. If you only want some advice as part of doing your own divorce, ask ahead of time to see if they are willing to do this and find out what their rates are for consultations. Most attorneys will do the first interview for nothing or a very small fee, perhaps $15 to $25. Hourly rates run from $50 to $200 per hour, but $100 is pretty common. Price is not everything — it has to feel right. Talk to the attorney and see if you like the experience.

13. Some Common Questions and Answers

a) **How much will it cost to do your own divorce?** The filing fees are set from time to time by law, and costs vary slightly from one county to another. These days, it costs around $180 to file papers in a case where your spouse signs a Waiver of the Citation, and about $10 more if the Citation must be issued, plus the Sheriff's fee (about $60) for serving the Citation on your spouse. Add to this a few dollars for photocopies and postage, and that's it. If you were to hire an attorney, you would have to pay these charges in addition to the lawyer's fee, so you will be paying them in any event.

b) **How long will it take?** The shortest possible time to complete a divorce is 61 days from the filing of the Petition, but plan on a bit longer, say three months. It is okay to take longer if you are in no hurry.

c) **What if we reconcile?** If you file a divorce Petition and later reconcile and change your mind, just let it lie there. Within a few months it will be dismissed for lack of prosecution, after a written notice from the clerk.

d) **When can we remarry?** After your final Decree of divorce is ordered you must wait at least 30 days before marrying anyone other than the spouse you just divorced.

e) **What about alimony?** In September of 1995 Texas finally joined the other 49 states in granting alimony (also called spousal maintenance) upon divorce. It is a stingy little law, and as with any new procedure, it is best left to attorneys until the wrinkles are ironed out. We include instructions for how to request alimony, but can't guarantee they will work. You still have the option of reaching an agreement with your spouse about alimony and making it part of a marital settlement agreement. This method is much more flexible, and the courts are used to it. See Chapter D, Support, for more detail.

f) **What if the wife is pregnant?** You should wait until the child is born to get your divorce. Judges do not like to see a child born out of wedlock and enforcing child support could be a problem. If you can't wait, see an attorney.

g) **Am I liable for my spouse's bills?** During the marriage (even if you are separated), both spouses are liable for the bills of the other. After the divorce, the parties are responsible only for their own bills.

h) **What if I am common-law married?** Three elements must exist to form a common-law marriage: 1) an agreement to be married (whether explicit or implied); 2) after the agreement you lived together as husband and wife; and 3) you represented to others that you were husband and wife. If your marriage is common-law, the same rules for divorce apply to you as to couples ceremonially married. However, if you believe you are common-law married, you have only two years from the date you separate to file for divorce. If neither party files within that time, it is presumed that no common-law marriage existed, and you won't be able to use this book to get a divorce.

i) **Does divorce have tax consequences?** Yes. Almost every aspect of divorce could possibly have important tax consequences. Depending upon what property and income you have, you could possibly save a lot of money by seeing a tax expert, especially before making a Marital Settlement Agreement. There are also rules you should know about if you have children. The tax rules are numerous and they change frequently, but fortunately there is an excellent little booklet that tells you everything you should know, and it is absolutely free. Simply call your local Internal Revenue Service office and ask for IRS publication 504, "Tax Information for Divorced or Separated Individuals."

B. Dividing the Property and Bills

One of the most important parts of a divorce action is dividing the property and debts (the estate) of the marriage. One of the most important services of an attorney is going over your estate with you to see what you own, what you owe, and how it can all be divided. The attorney will have an eye to getting you, the client, the best deal possible. Unless you have a large or complicated estate, this book will tell you how to understand your own estate and decide for yourself how to divide it.

1. Cases Where There Is No Property

Do not conclude that you have no property without going over the checklist in section 3 to make sure that you have thought of everything.

Cases without property are very easy to do because you merely tell the court that there is no significant property to be divided, and the court does nothing. There will be but little inquiry into your property and no orders about it.

Several types of cases can be handled this way. Perhaps there isn't enough property to worry about; say, where you own little more than your few personal possessions. Or, maybe your spouse is long gone, doesn't care and has abandoned what little property there is to you. Or, maybe you have already divided things between you, so at the time you file there is nothing left to be divided by the court. In cases like these, you may decide that you do not need or want the court to make orders about the division of your property.

Do not use this approach if there is any chance of future argument about property of any significant value, or where there is real estate that has not yet been divided correctly, or where there is a community interest in a pension plan.

2. Cases Where There Is Some Property

Make sure you understand your marital estate and know all that it contains. Read section 3 and go over the checklist very carefully to make sure you have thought of everything. Be sure to include property acquired anywhere else that would have been community property had it been acquired in Texas. If you think it likely that your spouse has hidden assets that you don't know and can't find out about, then you might benefit from the services of an attorney who can get the spouse in court and under order to reveal everything.

If at the time of your divorce your estate contains property or bills of any significant value, then you will want to have things divided properly as part of the divorce.

Property can be divided by the parties or by the judge. Spouses can agree to divide their property any way they see fit. If this is completed before the Petition is filed, then there is no community property to divide and the case will be very easy to conduct. If there is some community property but no agreement at the time of filing, then the property must be listed in the Petition. If by the time of the court hearing there is still no agreement, the property will be divided by the judge. In this case, neither spouse will be entirely in control of how the property gets divided, although the judge will be strongly influenced by the suggestions of the Petition or the spouse in court.

When thinking about dividing your property, keep in mind that getting the last cent may not be your best or highest goal. Consider the children, if any, the relative earning ability of each of you, your general situation, fairness and other such things. Try to consider what will be best for everyone, both now and in the future.

If you have a lot of property, you might want to think about getting professional advice from an accountant or lawyer. A professional can tell you how to locate it, value it, divide it, transfer it, and generally protect your interests. How much is "a lot" depends in part on how concerned you are about whatever you happen to have.

3. *Understanding Your Estate*

a. The marital estate: separate property and community property defined:

The marital estate is composed of the community marital estate (community property)—including property acquired anywhere else that would have been community had it been acquired in Texas—and the separate marital estates (separate property), if any, owned by the wife and by the husband individually. The character of property is typically determined at the time it was acquired, in particular by any title document.

Only community property needs to be divided, since separate property already belongs to each spouse individually. However, it makes sense to list items of significant value or personal meaning to make it clear that they are separate. This listing is done either in a written agreement between the spouses or in your Petition.

Separate property belongs just to one spouse and not the community. Separate property is property that was owned before marriage, *and* property that at any time came directly to just one spouse by gift or inheritance.

Community property belongs to both spouses equally. Community property is anything acquired by either spouse during the marriage, *in any state,* that is not separate property. Property possessed at the time of divorce by either spouse is presumed to be community property unless it can be shown to be otherwise by clear and convincing evidence. Even if the spouses have been separated for years, the earnings and debts of each spouse are community property until the divorce is ordered.

b. When funds flow between marital estates

During marriage, it is not uncommon for funds to flow between marital estates, that is, from separate to community or vice-versa. Unless there is a pre- or post-marital contract that states otherwise, then to the extent it can be made clear with records, one marital estate might have a claim against another marital estate for reimbursement, or perhaps a claim for economic contribution which matures on dissolution of the marriage. This subject can be technical and intricate, so if your case involves potential claims for reimbursement or equitable contribution, you might consider getting legal advice from a family law specialist.

Reimbursement. One marital estate can be asked to reimburse the other if one marital estate has paid the *un*secured liabilities of another marital estate; or if there has been inadequate compensation for the time, talent, and effort of a spouse by a business entity under the control of that spouse. Claims for reimbursement may be offset against each other if the parties can agree or a court determines it to be appropriate. Benefits for the use and enjoyment of property may be offset against a claim for reimbursement for expenditures to benefit a marital estate on property that does *not* involve a claim for economic contribution to the property.

Nonreimbursable claims. The court will not recognize a marital estate's claim for reimbursement for:
1. the payment of child support, alimony, or spousal maintenance;
2. the living expenses of a spouse or child of a spouse;
3. contributions of property of a nominal value;
4. the payment of a liability of a nominal amount; or
5. a student loan owed by a spouse.

Economic contribution. For example, there would be economic contribution if one spouse owned a house before marriage and during marriage the income of either spouse was used to pay the mortgage; or if the separate estate of either spouse was used to pay the mortgage of the community home.

In general, economic contribution is the dollar value by which equity in a property of one marital estate has been increased by contributions from another marital estate, either by reducing the principal of a debt secured by that property, or by funding capital improvements to the extent the value is increased. "Equity" means the fair market value of the property on a specific date, minus the amount of all lawful liens specific to the property on that same date. A claim for economic contribution does not cancel another claim for reimbursement. In the case of a conflict between a claim for economic contribution and a claim for reimbursement, the claim for economic contribution, if proven, prevails.

Property checklist and worksheet

Item	Market value	Amount owed	Net value	Proposed division

1. Real Estate
    family home
    rental property
    recreation property
    other				

2. Household goods, furniture and appliances				
3. Jewelry, antiques, art, collections, coins, etc.				
4. Vehicles, boats, trailers (get license and ID numbers)				
5. Cash on hand, and savings, checking, credit union accounts (get account numbers)				

B. Dividing the Property and Bills

Item	Market value	Amount owed	Net value	Proposed division
6. Life insurance with cash value (get policy numbers)				
7. Equipment, machinery, and livestock				
8. Stocks, bonds, secured notes				
9. Retirement/pension plans, profit-sharing plans, annuities				
10. Tax refunds due, accounts receivable, unsecured notes				
11. Partnerships, business interests				
12. Other assets				

13. List all other debts, taxes due, bills:

To whom due   **What for**   **Balance**

More specifically, in legal terms, economic contribution is the dollar amount of:
1. the reduction of the principal amount of a debt that existed at the time of marriage and that is secured by a lien on property owned before marriage;
2. the reduction of the principal amount of a debt that existed at the time of marriage and that is secured by a lien on property that was received by a spouse by gift or inheritance during a marriage;
3. the reduction of the principal amount of that part of a debt, including a home equity loan, that was (a) incurred during marriage; (b) secured by a lien on property; and (c) incurred for the acquisition of, or for capital improvements to, property;
4. the reduction of the principal amount of a debt that was (a) incurred during marriage; (b) secured by a lien on property owned by a spouse; (c) for which the creditor agreed to look for repayment solely to the separate marital estate of the spouse on whose property the lien attached; and (d) incurred for the acquisition of, or capital improvements to, property;
5. the refinancing of the principal amount described above, to the extent the refinancing reduces that principal amount; and
6. capital improvements to property other than by incurring debt.

Exclusions. Economic contribution does not include (1) expenditures for ordinary maintenance and repair or for taxes, interest, or insurance; or (2) the contribution by a spouse of time, toil, talent, or effort during the marriage.

Amount. A marital estate that makes an economic contribution to property owned by another marital estate has a claim for economic contribution with respect to the benefited estate. The amount of the claim is calculated by this formula:

$$E^d \; x \; \frac{C^c}{C^c + E^m + C^b}$$

Which in English terms, is equal to the product of:

$E^d =$ the equity in the benefited property on the date of dissolution; multiplied by a fraction of which the numerator is:

$C^c =$ the economic contribution to the property by the contributing estate; and the denominator is the sum of:

$C^c =$ the economic contribution to the property by the contributing estate;

$E^m =$ the equity in the property as of the date of the marriage or, if later, the date of the first economic contribution by the contributing estate; and

$C^b =$ the economic contribution to the property by the benefited estate during the marriage.

The amount of a claim may be less than the total of the economic contributions made by the contributing estate, but may not cause the contributing estate to owe funds to the benefited estate; nor can it exceed the equity in the property on the date of dissolution. The use and enjoyment of property during marriage does not create a claim of an offsetting benefit against the claim.

The claim for economic contribution does not does not affect the right to manage, control, or dispose of marital property. It does not create an ownership interest in property, but it does create a claim against the property of the benefited estate by the contributing estate. On dissolution of a marriage, the court will impose an equitable lien on property of a marital estate to secure a claim for economic contribution in that property by another marital estate. Subject to homestead restrictions, an equitable lien can be imposed on the entirety of a spouse's property in the marital estate and is not limited to the item of property that benefited from an economic contribution.

c. Bills and liabilities of the spouses

If there are bills owed by you and your spouse that were accumulated during your marriage, they will have to be valued and divided along with the property.

One thing you must understand is that orders of the court and agreements between the spouses about who is to pay bills do not in any way affect the people you owe — they are strictly between the spouses. If you owed money to someone before the divorce, and your spouse is ordered to pay the bill but does not do it, then you still owe the money. The creditor can come after you or repossess the property. Your spouse may be in contempt of court, for all the good that does you.

Between marriage and divorce, the spouses are liable for each other's debts. This means that if your spouse moved away five years ago, hasn't been heard from since, and bought some shoes last month, the shoe store can come to you for payment if the bill is not paid by your spouse. This unnecessary and unfortunate rule is the reason many people are in a big hurry to get their divorce over with.

As soon as you separate, close all joint accounts and notify all creditors in writing that you will no longer be responsible for the debts of your spouse.

d. Pension and retirement plans

There are often valuable benefits to employment beyond wages paid. These include accrued rights in a profit-sharing plan, retirement or pension plan, stock-option plan, employee savings plan, accrued unpaid bonuses, and so on. If either spouse was a participant in any

such plan during the marriage, then some part of that plan is community property. A community interest in any kind of plan *must* be dealt with as part of the divorce.

This area can be a real can of worms. If you read through the material below and get confused, don't feel bad — it confuses most lawyers too! Push through to the end where we make some practical suggestions about how to deal with your community interest in a pension plan.

Social Security is not community property and not subject to division by a court. It is a federal program with its own rules, so contact the Social Security Administration about your rights after divorce. Note that benefits accrue to spouses of a marriage that lasted at least ten years. If you are approaching the ten-year deadline, beware of losing benefits by rushing into a divorce that could conveniently be postponed.

Military and Federal Pensions: Military retirement pay and federal civil service benefits can be community property and subject to adjudication in state courts. Spouses of marriages that last through ten years or more of military service gain advantages in the enforcement of pension awards. Former spouses of marriages that lasted through at least twenty years of active military service are entitled to commissary and PX benefits. Don't be hasty with your divorce if you are approaching a 10- or 20-year deadline. Note also that a retiring military spouse can be bound to a written agreement to designate a former spouse as beneficiary under a Survivor Benefit Plan (SBP) if the agreement is incorporated, ratified or approved in a court order incident to a divorce, and if the Secretary concerned receives a request from the former spouse along with the agreement and court order.

What is the community interest worth? The many different kinds of pension plans have one thing in common — they are almost all extremely difficult to value before payments are actually due. Who knows what will happen between the present and the time the employee reaches retirement age? Correct valuation of the current value of a future pension right can only be done by an expert, usually a professional actuary who specializes in pensions, but there are very few of these around. If you call around to find one, be sure to ask them if they do "present buy-out appraisals of community interest in a pension plan." You might also ask them about how many they do each year. Most lawyers would not be capable of doing it right, nor would most accountants.

If your marriage was short, or employment meager and irregular, there may not be enough community interest in a pension fund to worry about. On the other hand, if your marriage lasted through long years of contributions to a pension fund, then perhaps you should seek expert assistance. One thing you can do on your own is write to the managers of the plan and ask when benefits become due, what amounts have been contributed to the employee's account, and what amount is due in the event of immediate termination. Ask if they can estimate the current worth of the employee's interest in the pension plan.

The community share in a pension plan is equal to the number of married years the employee-spouse was part of the plan, divided by the total number of years of service at the time of retirement. You multiply the current worth of the pension plan by this ratio to determine the current value of the community interest in the pension plan — that is the amount that is subject to division at the time of divorce.

How to deal with a pension plan when doing your own divorce: If you are listed as a beneficiary under your spouse's plan, you have the right to contact the plan administrator directly to find out just what the plan is worth. A good attorney can do a better job than you can at securing your rights by getting an expert evaluation, and by legally joining the pension plan as a party in your divorce, thus binding them to whatever orders the court makes regarding your interests. Joinder of the pension plan is the best way, but too complicated for you to do on your own. Going to an attorney may be very expensive now, but you have to weigh this against possible value to you in the future. A little pension money could mean a great deal to you later, and over a period of years it could add up. If you think your rights in a pension plan may be of significant value or importance to you, you should seek professional assistance to secure your maximum rights with maximum certainty. If you want to do it yourself, you can use the methods below either to settle the matter now or to put it off for later.

i) **Trade-off or waiver:** By this method, the employee spouse gets the half of the community share to which the non-employee spouse is entitled, thus having it all, and the non-employee spouse gets some other community property of a value equal to the share that was given up. This is most often an interest in the family home, but it could also be a promissory note (due on a certain date, or when benefits become payable). This kind of arrangement should be done as part of written Marital Settlement Agreement (see Chapter E), or by listing the pension in the Petition and dividing it in court along with all the other property.

If there is not enough other community property for a trade-off, and if no note is exchanged, then the non-employee spouse can simply waive (give up) all interest just to have the matter settled. This only makes sense if your interest isn't worth much, or if you have plenty of other resources. The Petitioner can make an oral waiver at the hearing, but at an uncontested hearing the Respondent does not appear, so any waiver from Respondent must be part of a written agreement (Chapter E) or in the form of a written waiver to be presented at the hearing by the Petitioner. It should say something like: "I,_____, am fully aware that there is or may be a community interest in my spouse's pension plan #A5S22A at

Acme Co., Austin, Texas. After giving it careful thought I have decided that I do not need nor want any part of it. I hereby waive any and all right which I may have to said pension plan. (Signed) (Date)." Although not necessary, having it notarized could have good effect.

ii) **Put it off:** Another way to deal with a pension is to ask the judge to reserve jurisdiction to fix the rights of the parties at some time in the future. If and when the employee-spouse first gets the right to retire and collect benefits, the whole matter becomes much more clear and easier to deal with. Then, or at any other time, either spouse can come back into court with a motion to have the matter settled. You should also have the judge order the employee-spouse not to apply for or accept benefits without first notifying the other spouse and applying to the court for a determination and division of community interest in the plan. If you do not ask the court to reserve jurisdiction, you will lose the right to ask for a division of a retirement asset if you do not pursue it within two years.

If, after reading this section, you are still uncertain about your rights, then you should see an attorney or CPA, at least for advice. The problem is that a great many professionals don't know much about it either. Ask before you go in.

e. The family home and other real estate

If you and your spouse own or have been buying your own home or other real property at the time of the divorce, then you must decide how to divide it. Some of the likely alternatives are to:

- sell it and split the proceeds; or

- have one spouse transfer it outright to the other; or

- have one spouse transfer it to the other in return for something, such as other property, or a note for some amount to be paid in the future (at some specific date or upon some specified event, such as when the kids are grown, if and when the house is sold, the spouse moves out of it, or any other that you can agree to).

When thinking about what to do with your family home or other real property, you will want to know how much of it you actually own — this amount is called your "equity." Your equity in any property is the difference between what you can get for it on the current market less any amounts due on it and the costs of selling it. You can best find out the current market value of your property by consulting a professional real estate appraiser. This will cost some money, so call around for prices. You would also do fairly well by calling in a few local real estate agents, but this may not be quite as accurate. Once you have figured the market value, deduct the amounts you owe on it and the commission for the real estate agents. If you don't sell it yourself, they will get six to eight percent. Add on a few hundred dollars for miscellaneous expenses.

The divorce will be much easier if you can settle the matter of the real estate and transfer it before you file the Petition. That way you won't have to list the house and make orders about it in your Decree.

Agreements about real property are not enforceable unless they are in writing. In order to actually transfer the home from joint ownership by both spouses into sole ownership of one spouse, you need to make up a deed from one spouse to the other, then have that deed signed before a Notary and recorded in the county where the property is located. Similarly, if a note is to be assumed, then it too must be properly drawn up, signed, and recorded. There will be a small fee for recording and maybe a transfer tax. If you cannot make up your own deed or note from forms available at a stationer's, then you should seek assistance from a title company, bank, real estate broker, or attorney. Call around. A form for transferring the property between spouses is included with the forms in the back of this book.

If you do not transfer the home before the Petition is filed, then it must be listed with your other property. If it is still not transferred by the time of the hearing, or settled by written agreement of the spouses, then the judge will divide it along with all the other listed property. In the Petition and Decree the property should be listed by both its common address and legal description (as on the deed). The judge can award the house to one spouse, or order it sold and the proceeds divided in some particular way. It is much better if the spouses take care of it their own way before the Petition is filed.

The time and manner of transfer could possibly have tax consequences such that it would benefit both spouses to cooperate over the transfer to arrange it to their own advantage. See a tax expert if you have enough income and property to benefit from tax games.

f. Income taxes

Any income taxes owed or refunds you are due should be divided along with the rest of your property. Most people split these 50-50, but you can agree to any division you want. If you settle division of taxes in a Marital Settlement Agreement (see Chapter E), you do not need to list them in your Decree.

You will also need to decide how to divide any income taxes that you *will owe* or refunds you *will receive* for the year of the divorce itself. The easiest way is to agree that each of you will be responsible for taxes incurred on his or her own income only. If your divorce is completed before December 31, you will file taxes as "single" or "head of household."

If you do not have your Decree by December 31, you have the option of filing as "married filing jointly" or "married filing separately." If you and your spouse are in agreement, work up the tax forms both ways to see which form of filing is most advantageous to both of you and share the benefit.

Keep in mind that if you and your spouse owe back taxes the IRS may still hold you liable even if the debt is assigned to your spouse in your divorce. Tax problems are beyond the scope of this book. You should contact a tax lawyer, CPA or an enrolled IRS agent before you go to court if you have questions.

4. When Property Is Divided by the Court

If there is any community property, or debts of any significance at the time of your divorce, then your estate must be properly divided. Property can be divided either by agreement of the spouses, or by the judge according to his or her own standards. There are many advantages to working things out by agreement. These are discussed in section B5, but first it might help to understand how things work when left to the court to divide.

Where there is any significant property apart from personal possessions that is not divided by the time the Petition is filed, then *all* the valuable property and debts of the spouses should be listed in the Petition. The Petition should indicate which is community and which is separate property. It is also a very good idea to indicate how the Petitioner wishes the property and debts to be divided.

If there is still no agreement by the time of the hearing, then the court has almost complete discretion as to how it will order the property divided. The law states only that the court must divide the property in a manner that it thinks just and right, considering the rights of the spouses and children. This leaves things pretty wide open for anything to happen. The court will consider the property, the children, earning ability of each spouse, and any other circumstances the judge thinks relevant, then make a decision which is extremely difficult to reverse. The judge will be very strongly influenced by the Petition and by the words of the Petitioner at the hearing, and very likely will decide as requested. But there is no guarantee of this. Even attorneys are sometimes surprised by the judge's decision.

The judge will usually divide *only* the community property, and will not touch the separate property. However, in rare cases where it seems necessary, the judge may invade a spouse's separate property for the benefit of children.

Here are some general rules of thumb for you to consider, but you must keep in mind that there is no certainty as to what kind of order a judge will make.

a) An approximately equal division of the property and debts will most likely be ordered where there are no children and the spouses have equal earning abilities and equal circumstances. This is especially true in short marriages. In such cases, where an item has a debt attached to it, as where it was mortgaged or bought on time, the spouse getting the item will most often get the debt too.

b) An unequal division of the property and debts may be ordered in favor of the spouse with:

- custody of the child(ren)
- greater need,
- lesser earning ability, or
- favorable circumstances of fairness.

Where there are children, the family home and furnishings are most always kept together for the benefit of the children and awarded to the spouse with custody. The wage-earner spouse may be ordered to pay debts on items he or she does not possess (if he or she fails to pay, the creditor may come and get the stuff anyway).

If the court awards you property that is still in the possession of your spouse, you have to figure out how to get it. If you can't get it peacefully, then you will need an attorney to help you get it, if it is worth the money and trouble.

5. Dividing It By Agreement

If your property is minimal, then you can just go ahead and divide it up, and that will be that. Where there are items of any value, it is usually better to make some sort of written agreement just to help you keep track of what it was you actually agreed to. If there is any real estate, then the agreement must be in writing. If the Respondent is to give up rights to a pension plan, there must be something in writing to show the judge.

In uncontested divorces a judge will nearly always follow the agreement of the spouses, so long as it appears to be generally fair. But you should know that the judge is not legally bound to follow your contract, and especially in matters of child custody and support a judge will want to make sure that things are well and fairly arranged. For example, except in extreme cases, no judge would allow a mother to give up all child support, even if she wanted to, or allow a welfare recipient to give up property without a very good reason.

Chapter E discusses written agreements and shows you two ways to go about making one.

6. How to Transfer Titles to Property

A certain kind of property is not merely owned, but rather is held under some sort of document or written indicator of ownership, called "title." This includes real estate; motor vehicles, boats, and trailers; bank accounts, stocks, and bonds. In such cases, ownership after divorce is not complete until title has been properly transferred or otherwise dealt with.

As with every other part of your divorce, it is always much easier if your spouse will cooperate with you. If this is not possible, you can usually accomplish your goal some other way, but not always.

If your spouse is not cooperative, then getting title is merely the first step — you still have to get possession. In some cases it means a lot to have possession first, as with bank accounts that could be spent while you are waiting around to get title. If you cannot get possession in any peaceful way, you may have to seek the help of an attorney or give it up.

a. Real estate is easy to transfer if your spouse will sign a warranty deed, which is included with the forms in the back of this book. The deed is then recorded at the

Clerk's Office in the county where the land is located. There will be a very nominal recording fee of a few dollars. It is very helpful to have this done before the hearing, possibly even before you file the Original Petition.

If the transfer is not made by the time you file your Petition, then you must list it, being careful to use the exact legal description of the property, which you can copy from your deed. The deed is on file at the Clerk's Office in the county where the land is located. If the transfer is still not voluntarily made by the time of your hearing, then the property must be awarded as part of the Decree, still with the entire legal description. If the land is in Texas, title can be transferred merely by filing a certified copy of the Decree with the Clerk's Office in the county where the land is located. If the land is not in Texas then the order of the Texas court will probably not serve to transfer it. Instead, all you can do is to make sure that the Decree very specifically orders your spouse personally to make a transfer by deed to you. Then you have to try to enforce the order by contempt proceedings. This will require the service of an attorney.

b. Vehicles can be transferred by a cooperative spouse merely by the signing of the form on the back of the vehicle title slip. You can also have your spouse sign a Power of Attorney to Transfer Motor Vehicle in front of a notary public. This document gives whoever receives the car the power to transfer it. You will find a copy of this form is in the back of this book. You should take this in to the auto transfers office in your county within ten working days of the date of the signature. If the title slip has been lost, you will need to pick up a special form at that office to replace the lost one.

If your spouse will *not* cooperate, then the vehicle must be listed and awarded to you in the Decree. The description must be very complete, including make, model, year, license plate number, and motor or vehicle I.D. number. Take a certified copy of the Decree to the auto transfers office and they will have you fill out a couple of forms, pay a few dollars, and the transfer will be made.

Any way you do it, if there is a lien on the auto (where you owe money on it), the lien must be brought forward on the new title.

c. Bank accounts are commonly held in one of three ways: (i) an individual name, (ii) in the names of "H or W," (iii) in the names of "H and W."

If the account is in your own individual name, it is yours and you don't have to worry about it. If it is in the individual name of your spouse, then even an attorney would have a hard time doing much about it. The easiest thing to do is to list it on the Petition at its value at that time, and have it awarded to your spouse as a set-off for something else that you want.

If the account is in the name of you *or* your spouse, as is most common, this means either one of you can withdraw it at any time. You might want to take out as much as you wish to protect and put it into an account in your own name.

Joint accounts in the name of one spouse *and* the other are probably very rare. This would mean that the signature of *both* spouses is required to make a transfer. In such a case, if your spouse will not cooperate, take a certified copy of the divorce Decree to the bank and see if that does the trick. If not, a court order will be required and you will need an attorney's services to get it. Until then, the money is safe, since your spouse can't get it either.

This discussion applies also to other types of property and instruments, such as stocks and bonds which, like bank accounts, can be held individually or jointly. Possession of the paper means a great deal, especially with "bearer" instruments such as government bonds, which can be negotiated by whoever has possession.

d. Tax refunds are easy with the cooperation of your spouse, and fairly easy in any event if you have possession of the refund check. Either get your spouse's signature when and where required, or take the check along with a certified copy of the divorce Decree down to the nearest IRS office. If you do not have possession of the check, then use your innate cunning to get it peacefully, or forget it. A lawyer has a few tricks that sometimes work, but it's rarely worth it, since the check is usually not even big enough to pay the lawyer's fee.

e. Insurance policies can be transferred merely by sending the insurance company a certified copy of the Decree awarding the policy or any covered property to you.

C. Children: Custody and Visitation

1. Generally

The divorce Petition *must* list all children of the marriage under the age of 18 and not married. This means any child natural-born to both spouses or adopted by both. You should include stepchildren only if legally adopted by the stepparent. Any child born to the wife at any time between marriage and divorce is strongly presumed to be her husband's. If this is not the case, you should get an attorney to handle your case and straighten out the child's paternity.

If the custody of any child has ever come before a Texas court, then you will have to have an attorney handle your case. It is too complicated to handle a case like this yourself. If you are unsure about this—if there is even the slightest chance that there has been a Texas court involved with the child's custody—then you should make a formal inquiry like this: write to the Texas Department of Human Resources at 701 W. 51st Street, Austin, TX 78759; give them the full name and birthdate of each child; request to know "the court of continuing jurisdiction, if any" for each child listed. If they send back the information that the child is not under the jurisdiction of any court, then you are free to go ahead with your case, but *be sure* you take their response to the hearing with you and put it into evidence.

All orders about custody, visitation, and support of children are subject to modification. If circumstances change, either parent can go back into court at any time after one year to seek a change in the court orders.

When you have children, a divorce never completely ends the relationship between you and your spouse. You no longer live together, but chances are you will see and hear from each other because of the children. This makes it extremely important that you try to keep things as calm and pleasant as possible. It is not good for the children or for their parents if you can't get over your differences at least enough to permit the parental relationship to continue and grow.

Managing and Possessory Conservators: Sometimes it's easy to believe that lawmakers have a special department packed with full-time bureaucrats whose sole job is to figure out how to make simple things sound very complicated. For some unimaginable reason, Texas law calls the parent with custody the "managing conservator" and the other parent (the one that visits) is called the "possessory conservator." What used to be called "visitation" is now called "possession." It takes practice, but you will get the hang of it, eventually.

2. Custody

There are two forms of custody for children in Texas. The preferred method, as decreed by the Texas Legislature, is *joint managing conservatorship* or JMC. In a joint conservatorship, the parents continue to share the duties and responsibilities of raising the child(ren), just like during a marriage. However, those duties and responsibilities are spelled out very specifically in your Decree, so you can tailor your conservatorship to fit the agreement between you and your spouse.

JMC does *not* necessarily mean equal or even near equal periods of possession. It also does not eliminate the requirement for child support. In a joint conservatorship, one parent is selected to provide the primary residence, or domicile, for the child. We will call this parent the "domicile parent."

The second custody form is *sole managing/possessory conservatorship.* In this arrangement, one parent is awarded primary custody and responsibilities, while the other parent has more limited duties and visitation (possession). This custody arrangement, which used to be the norm, should now only be used when you can show the judge that joint custody is not in the best interest of your child(ren). Some examples of reasons while sole managing conservatorship may be preferred include: the other parent cannot be located; a parent has a history of substance abuse; the other parent committed family violence against you or the children; or a parent whose physical or mental disabilities could harm the child. Judges may be reluctant to order sole managing conservatorship, so put together strong evidence to bring to court when you have your hearing.

Generally, judges have the discretion to structure custody, visitation and support in ways they feel are in the child's best interest. Because the laws covering these issues are so detailed nowadays, judges will want to have a very good reason for deviating from them. Unfortunately, because you are doing your own divorce, some judges will scrutinize your divorce Decree much more carefully than one brought to them by a lawyer. That is why we provide you with detailed instructions and orders to include in your Decree.

These general principles will give you an idea of what the judge will usually order:

- Parents are preferred over third parties.
- Although both parents are supposed to be considered equal, a preference is usually given to the mother, particularly when there are young children involved. A father can win custody easier when the children are older or it is clear that the mother is unfit.
- Split custody (one for me and two for you) is to be avoided.

- Children twelve years of age and older can express a preference in writing for which parent they with to live with. Generally, a judge will go along with the child's choice, but is not required to. The judge can interview the child in chambers, and will certainly do so if the matter is contested.

While Texas has come a long way in changing its attitude, the maternal preference still prevails. Yes, it is sexist. Yes, it is unfair to fathers. But this is the way it is in the majority of courts in Texas.

In most cases where there is a custody battle, a social study of the family will be ordered. Some nice social worker type of person will "study" your family and talk to everyone you know and don't know to find out what is best for your child(ren), then make a report to the court. The lawyers on each side will probably try to make the other side look like a disaster for the kids, and there's even a chance that an older child could end up on the witness stand. Whoever wins, the kids usually lose. Don't do it unless you have no other choice. It is much better to work it out outside of court, if you can do it peacefully. In tough cases, consider using a trusted friend, member of the clergy, mediator, or counselor for help.

You would be foolish to attempt to be your own lawyer if your spouse opposes you legally.

3. Visitation (Possession)

In a joint managing conservatorship the parent who provides the primary residence for the children has domicile rights. The other parent will have regular possession of (visitation with) the children. "Visitation" is called "possession" in Texas, perhaps because the idea of being merely a visitor increases the visiting parent's sense of distance from the child. We use both terms in this book, but in court and in conversations with your spouse you should remember to talk about shared "possession."

During the time the parent without "domicile" rights actually possesses the child, the rights and duties of that parent are spelled out by law. Read the Decree in Chapter 7 carefully to see just how these rights and duties are defined. You and your spouse should discuss these issues and decide which duties and responsibilities you will share and which will be reserved for only one parent.

Divorce is not the end of the relationship between spouses who have children. There is still the continuing need (a duty, in fact) for both parents to be involved regularly in the lives of their children. Studies have shown that children of divorced parents are most badly damaged when hard feelings and steady fighting continue long after the divorce. Children adjust fairly well if the heat and smoke clear away soon after the Decree, so it is very important to make your co-parenting as smooth and comfortable as possible.

"Reasonable visitation" was once ordered in most cases, but it is no longer favored because it leaves the parents entirely on their own to work out the details of the schedule of who has the kids when. This is too difficult when parents are not getting along well. Vast experience has shown that parents and children are far better off when visitation is ordered in great detail, so everyone knows exactly what the minimum standards are. Parents can actually work visitation any way they like by agreement, without regard for the terms of the Decree. But, whenever relations become strained, then the specific visitation terms will define the schedule very clearly, and there's less to argue about.

To keep things clear, the divorce Decree uses the terms most familiar to judges for possession: "Managing Conservator" and "Possessory Conservator" or MC and PC. Note that these terms do not change your joint custody; they are merely shorthand "legalese."

Texas has statewide standard terms for possession (visitation) that are, by law, presumed to be in the child's best interest. This means that in most cases these guidelines, or something very close to them, must be part of any Decree involving the custody of children. The standard terms for possession are included with the rest of the forms in the back of this book. They can be torn out and filed with your Decree. They will seem very intricate at first, but will become clearer after careful study, so take a close look.

In JMC, the Standard Possession Order is presumed to be the *minimum* amount of possession for the visiting parent. You can add additional dates to it. Some parents use the Standard Possession Order rigidly, while others prefer to change visits regularly. It is advisable for the children's sake that once you settle on dates and times, you stick closely to them. Children require stability to feel secure. It would be very unsettling for you not to know until Friday where you were spending the night — think about how your child feels!

You can alter the terms to fit work schedules of the parents or other special needs of the parents or child, so long as you stay close to the standard terms. But there are only two ways to get completely different terms. The parties can enter into a written agreement with almost any reasonable terms they like, subject to the court's approval. Absent agreement, if the court is given a very good reason it can find that the guidelines are unworkable or unreasonable under your special circumstances and something completely different can be ordered. The parent who has custody is not allowed to forbid visiting merely because the support money is not coming in or because the parents are angry with one another. Visitation is not a weapon to be used against the visiting spouse.

Visitation problems. Effective June 2001, counties are authorized to set up visitation centers to facilitate visitation or exchange. Check with your county to see if they have this service. If they do, pay them a visit to discuss how they can help you.

You should know that there are criminal sanctions against a person who keeps or conceals a child in order to frustrate visitation orders. For example, if the visiting parent just decides to keep the child for awhile and not bring the child home when due, there would be a strong reaction indeed from the authorities, if you were to take the matter before them.

In some very rare cases, it may be clear that it is dangerous to permit any visitation at all. You will have to show the court strong evidence that some specific harm is likely to come to the children if visitation of any kind is allowed. This means clearly showing a pattern of behavior such as heavy use of drugs or alcohol, sexual abuse, or violence toward the children. If you are determined to prevent visitation altogether you would be better off with an attorney.

4. Agreements

The court is very likely to honor a written agreement of the parties concerning conservatorship and possession (visitation), so long as it appears to be reasonable and in the best interest of the children. In such cases, the Decree will contain an order that sets out the same terms as the agreement. Even in your agreement, it is best to spell out the terms of possession as clearly and in as much detail as possible. Use the standard terms in the back of the book as a guide.

It is not at all common, but still possible, that the judge will find the agreement not in the best interest of the children. If this happens, the judge will either issue orders of his own design, or perhaps request the parties to submit a revised agreement.

5. Class Required for Parents?

Many counties in Texas now require that divorcing parents take a course on how divorce affects the children. Called something like "Helping Children Cope with Divorce" or "Putting Kids First," this course is part of a nationwide trend to soften the impact of divorce on children. Both parents must take this course and present proof to the judge at the final hearing. If you do not know where your spouse is, the court may waive the requirement that your spouse attend the class, but you will still have to attend. The course is four hours long and average cost is $30.

Counties requiring classes and class providers change frequently. Please call your court to find out if a course is required and who offers it. A schedule of dates, places, and times can be obtained at the District Clerk's office in each county or by calling 888-784-5437. At press time, we had the following information:

These counties require the class: Bandera, Blanco, Bosque, Burnet, Camp, Cass, Cherokee, Comanche, Coryell, Delta, Ellis, Fannin, Franklin, Gregg, Hamilton, Hopkins, Hunt, Johnson, Kendall, Kerr, Llano, Lubbock, Marion, Mason, Morris, Rains, Rockwall, San Saba, Smith, Somervell, Stephens, Titus, Upshur, Wood, and Young.

Classes are also offered in these counties but we do not know if they are required: Angelina, Collin, Fort Bend, Galveston, Grayson, Henderson, Howard, Kaufman, Lamar, Lampasas, Midland, Nacogdoches, Navarro, Nueces, Panola, Potter, Taylor, and Tom Green.

D. Support

Spousal Maintenance

For cases filed after September 1, 1995, Texas finally allows alimony, called spousal maintenance, but only in limited circumstances. You are eligible for alimony if:

- Within two years prior to filing the divorce, your spouse was convicted (or received deferred adjudication for) a "family violence offense;" *or*

- You were married at least ten years and will not have sufficient property after the divorce for your minimum reasonable needs; *and* you:
  - cannot support yourself because you are physically or mentally disabled; *or*
  - have primary conservatorship of a physically or mentally disabled child whose needs require you to stay at home to care for the child; *or*
  - lack the earning ability to provide for your minimum needs.

"Family violence offense" means an assault against you, your child or a family member, or a violation of a family violence protective order. Sometimes criminal mischief (vandalism), or terroristic threats are also considered family violence. If your spouse was convicted of some act and you are not sure it was "family violence," call the court where the conviction occurred and ask the court clerk. You will need a certified copy of the conviction to show the judge when you get your divorce.

Spousal maintenance cannot last more than three years. This is a very short window of opportunity to upgrade job skills and become employable again. Maintenance ends if you remarry or if you begin cohabiting in a conjugal relationship with another person. If you are permanently disabled, you may qualify for indefinite maintenance, subject to review of the court. The amount of maintenance will be the lesser of $2,500 per month or 20% of the paying spouse's monthly gross income.

Spousal support can be ordered for any amount and time period if both parties agree and the support order is incorporated into a written agreement (see Chapter E).

Health insurance

Under federal law (COBRA) spouses and children who will lose their health coverage due to divorce from the primary wage-earner are now entitled to continued coverage and benefits for up to three years at similar rates (100% of what the employer pays), but now at their own expense. The wage-earner may be required to pay for the insurance of the children (see below), but the spouse will have to pay for his or her own coverage. To exercise this right, you *must* give written notice of the divorce and your desire to continue coverage to the Plan Administrator within 60 days after your Decree is signed by the judge. The plan *cannot* insist on new evidence of insurability. Compare rates and coverage available to you under other alternatives before you decide.

If you are presently covered by a health plan provided through *your* employer and it provides coverage comparable to your spouse's plan, your spouse's employer is not required to offer you COBRA coverage. To be sure, contact the Plan Administrator at your spouse's company. They may want to see a copy of the policy your employer provides to decide whether you qualify for the COBRA option.

Child support

The obligation of a parent to support a child is natural, basic and imposed by law. All judges give it the highest priority. The duty lasts until the child reaches majority at age 18, or becomes emancipated by getting married or moving out and becoming self-supporting. If an unemancipated minor is fully enrolled in an accredited high-school program at age 18, support is extended to the end of the school year in which the child graduates. Support can be ordered beyond age 18 by agreement of the parents, or for children who became handicapped before the age of 18 and will not be capable of self-support. The obligation survives the death of the recipient and extends to whoever has the custody and care of the child.

Texas has statewide child support guidelines that judges are required to consider in every case. While not exactly mandatory, they are *presumed* to be reasonable and in the best interest of the child. Without a written agreement with your spouse, if you want to get a different amount ordered, you will have to present evidence (facts and figures) that show a good reason for departing from the guidelines. Then a court *may* decide that to apply the guides would be unfair or inappropriate under the circumstances and order a different amount. Here's how the guidelines work:

1. Framework for child support guidelines

a) The guidelines call for the **"obligor"** to pay a percentage of his or her **"monthly net resources"** to the **"obligee."**

b) The parents can agree to any amount of support, even if it varies from these guidelines, but subject to approval of the court. The court will probably approve any *reasonable* agreement of the parties.

c) On *written* request of either party within *10* days of the child support order, the judge must state the basis for the order, and if the award varied from the guidelines the reason(s) for the departure *must* be given.

d) The guidelines are applied without regard to gender of the obligor, obligee or child. In setting child support the judge may consider the needs of the child, the ability of the parent to contribute to the support of the child, any financial resources available for the support of the child and the amount of possession of and access to a child by the parties.

2. Definitions

The **"Obligor"** is the parent ordered to pay. The **"Obligee"** is the person who is to receive the child support.

To get **"monthly net resources,"** you first add up the **"gross monthly resources"** of the obligor, which is much broader than "income" as used for tax purposes. Gross resources includes all benefits from personal effort; *everything*— 100% of all wage and salary income *before* any deductions, and including overtime, commissions, tips, bonuses, interest, dividends, royalties, net rental income (deducting only operating expenses and mortgage payments but not non-cash items such as depreciation), and pensions, severance pay, trust income, annuities, capital gains, social security, disability or unemployment benefits, gifts, prizes and child support received under a court order. The *only* income *not* considered is welfare received for children.

When figuring income from self-employment (includes partnerships, joint ventures, close corporations), include all income and the value of benefits of any kind, allowing deductions only for ordinary expenses and amounts necessary to produce income, but not such things as depreciation, tax credits, or other non-cash deductions.

In cases where your spouse is gone, or for any other reason you are unable to get any information about his or her income, the law says wages shall be presumed to be equal to the prevailing federal minimum wage for a forty-hour week. You should go ahead and get your child support order with this figure and when income information becomes available, you will have a basis for filing for modification of child support. When you use this kind of order for a missing spouse, the Attorney General's office can get involved in trying to find the obligor to get the support paid.

"Monthly net resources" is critical, because support is figured as a percentage of the monthly net resources of the obligor. First, you add up the gross monthly resources (as defined above), then subtract the permitted deductions—social security taxes, union dues, expenses for health insurance coverage for the obligor's child(ren), and federal income tax withholding equal to that for a single person claiming one exemption and taking the standard deduction. It is sometimes best to figure resources and deductions on an annual basis, then divide by 12 for the average monthly figure.

The court can also consider any additional factors that increase or decrease the obligor's ability to pay. This includes valuable assets that do not produce an income, income-producing assets that have been voluntarily shifted to produce less income, and income that is significantly less than the obligor could earn because the obligor is voluntarily unemployed or underemployed. The court, in such cases, may apply the guidelines to the earning *potential* of the obligor.

3. Guidelines

The percentage of net monthly resources allocated to child support depends on the number of children to support from this marriage, as well as any children from a prior relationship the obligor is legally obligated to support.

In the table below, you use the *top line* to find the percentage of net monthly resources to calculate child support if the obligor does not have other children to support. Multiply the obligor's net monthly resources by the percentage under the number of children born to or adopted by you and your spouse.

If the obligor *does* have a legal obligation to support children from a previous relationship, use the number in the left hand column to find the number of children already supported, and follow it across the table to the number of children that are to be supported in the current case. This percentage of obligor's net monthly resources will be the total guideline child support for the children of *this* divorce.

		Number of children in this case						
		1	**2**	**3**	**4**	**5**	**6**	**7**
Number of	**0**	20.00%	25.00%	30.00%	35.00%	40.00%	40.00%	40.00%
other children	**1**	17.50	22.50	27.38	32.20	37.33	37.71	38.00
obligor has	**2**	16.00	20.63	25.20	30.33	35.43	36.00	36.44
a legal duty	**3**	14.75	19.00	24.00	29.00	34.00	34.67	35.20
to support	**4**	13.60	18.33	23.14	28.00	32.89	33.60	34.18
	5	13.33	17.86	22.50	27.22	32.00	32.73	33.33
	6	13.14	17.50	22.00	26.60	31.27	32.00	32.62
	7	13.00	17.22	21.60	26.09	30.67	31.38	32.00

The court will apply the guidelines to the obligor's first $6,000 of net monthly resources. If there is more, the court can order additional amounts of child support as appropriate, depending on the lifestyle of the family, income of the parties, and needs of the child(ren). In such cases, it might be wise to get advice from an attorney.

If the obligor receives social security old age benefits, subtract from the guideline support the value of benefits paid to the child through social security old age benefits.

Agreements of the spouses will be given great weight and consideration in court, but the judge has the power to make a different order if s/he thinks it is in the best interest of the child. The judge is especially likely to interfere if the support amount seems too low and the custodial parent also has low income.

4. Health Insurance

Health care coverage is considered an integral part of the child support obligation and *will* be ordered along with financial support. This something the judge *must* do.

a) If health insurance is available for the child through the obligor's employment or membership in a union, trade association, or other organization at reasonable cost, the court **shall** order the obligor to include the child in the obligor's health insurance.

b) If not available under (a) above, but available through the obligee's employment or membership in a union, trade association, or other organization at reasonable cost, the court **may** order the obligee to provide health insurance for the child and order the obligor to pay additional child support for the actual cost of the health insurance for the child.

c) If not available under (a) or (b) above, the court shall order the obligor to provide health insurance for the child if the court finds that health insurance is available to the obligor from another source at reasonable cost.

d) If neither parent has access to private health insurance at reasonable cost, the court shall order the custodial parent (or, to extent permitted by law, the non-custodial parent) to immediately apply on behalf of the child for participation in whatever public medical assistance program for which the child might be eligible, and that the obligor pay additional child support for the actual cost of such program.

e) If none of the above available, court shall order obligor to pay a reasonable amount (as determined by court) each month as medical support.

"Reasonable cost" means not over 10% of the responsible parent's net monthly income.

The court will require the parent ordered to provide health coverage to produce evidence to the court's satisfaction that the parent has applied for and/or secured health insurance, or has otherwise taken action to provide health care coverage, as ordered by the court. A parent ordered to provide health insurance who fails to do so is liable for necessary medical expenses of the child, and the cost of health insurance premiums, if an, paid on behalf of the child.

5. Factors the Court Will Consider in Evidence

In setting the amount of support, the court is expected to consider the *totality* of the circumstances. This means everything relevant, including, but not limited to:

a) the amount of the obligee's net resources, including the earning *potential* if the obligee is intentionally unemployed or underemployed, and any property the obligee may own;

b) the age and needs of the child;

c) child care expenses incurred by either party to maintain employment;

d) whether either party has custody or support of another child, and amounts actually being paid under another child support order;

e) whether either party has a car, housing, or other benefits furnished by an employer, a business, or another person;

f) other deductions from wages or other compensation of the parties;

g) cost of health care insurance and any uninsured medical expenses;

h) extraordinary educational, health care or other special expenses of the parties or of the child(ren);

i) cost of travel to exercise access to or possession of a child;

j) debts assumed by either party; and

k) whether social security, disability or SSI benefits are received by a party on behalf of the child(ren).

In cases where it seems appropriate, the judge has the power to order any parent's property set aside and administered in a trust for the benefit of the child. The court can also order any parent to make a lump-sum payment in addition to or in lieu of periodic payments. These are unusual steps, so if you wish something along these lines, you should consult an attorney.

When hearing your case, the court is likely to want income tax returns for the past two years and current wage stubs, so have these with you when you go to the hearing. Though not required, it is also a good idea to file or at least take with you a worksheet that shows the income of both spouses, and expenses of the custodial parent. We provide a Financial Information worksheet in the forms section at the back of the book that you can speak from, show to the judge or file with the court if you wish to.

6. Income withholding

An order for income withholding is required in every case where there is child support. It can also include amounts for spousal maintenance, but only if the recipient is the managing conservator of the child for whom support is owed and the child resides with him/her. Further, income withholding for spousal maintenance can be ordered if payments are imposed by a court, but there can be no withholding for spousal maintenance agreed by the parties unless the contract specifically permits it, or where payments under a contract have not been made in a timely fashion.

The withholding order remains on file with the court until you ask the clerk's office to "issue" it to the obligor's employer, and the court retains jurisdiction until all support is paid. Most courts charge a fee of about $15 to issue the order to the employer.

If the obligor is unemployed, self-employed or can't be located, you obviously need not bother having the order issued until circumstances change. You also have the option of agreeing not to have the order issued as long as support payments do not fall 30 days behind. In cases where the children are receiving public assistance, the withholding order must be issued.

After support is ordered, it still remains to be collected. Therefore, support in most counties must be paid through the local child support registry or through the Office of the Attorney General. Call the clerk's office in your county to find out the correct office name and address to use in your withholding order, then call that office to ask for an account number. Payment through the registry protects both parents because it gives an unbiased record of the payment amounts and dates received. If you are not receiving your child support, the Attorney General's office provides collection services, and larger counties have domestic relations offices that enforce child support for county residents. To enforce child support, tax returns can be intercepted, licenses can be suspended, wages can be garnished and the non-paying parent can be jailed.

The withholding order requires the name, address, and phone number of the obligor and the obligor's employer, if known, and the obligor's social security number and driver's license number, as well as social security numbers for the children. Each parent is required to give written notice to the other, to the court, and to the State Case

Registry Office 60 days in advance of any changes in this information. If you don't know 60 days in advance, you are required to notify the other party within 5 days of the date you find out. If you have some good reason why you don't want your spouse to know where you are, you do not have to list your own address in public documents.

Either party can come back into court at any time after one year to modify the support order. It would have to be shown that circumstances had changed markedly since the previous order was made. The Attorney General's Office provides a free review of child support for possible modification once every three years, or more often if there has been a change in circumstances. This service may also be available through the Domestic Relations Office in larger counties. Contact these offices for information.

7. Tax exemptions for the children

The IRS test for who qualifies to take the dependency exemption depends on who has provided the most financial support. The IRS usually presumes that the "domicile" parent, the one the child lived with most of the year, qualifies to take the exemption. The "non-domicile" parent can claim the exemption only if he or she contributed over half of the child's support *and* the domicile parent agrees to sign IRS Form 8332, which turns over the dependency exemption to the non-domicile parent. In families where the obligor earns a lot more than the obligee, it makes sense to do this, because the family will save on the obligor's taxes and can agree to share the tax savings the obligor realizes. Run the taxes both ways and share the amount saved.

E. Marital Settlement Agreements

We have several times discussed the impressive advantages of a divorce by agreement, and now it is at last time to show you how this is actually done.

Marital settlement agreements are subject to the approval of the court. Judges are especially likely to take a close interest in the arrangements you have made for the custody and support of your child(ren), if any. Still, assuming that the agreement appears to be generally fair, it is almost certain that it will be approved.

In matters of child support and custody, the court retains its power to modify its orders no matter what the agreement of the parties. This means that in the future, should circumstances change in some important way, either party can come back into court for a different order concerning the best interests of the minor children.

In order for a marital agreement to be enforceable in the future, it must fulfill two minimum conditions:

- The agreement must be generally fair.

- It must have been made without undue pressure, force, mistake, or fraud. No bullying or cheating, in other words.

We are going to show you two different ways to go about a divorce by agreement. The first is the Approved Decree, and then there is the full-blown Marital Settlement Contract.

1. The Approved Decree

This is an easy way to work out an agreed divorce. By this method, you prepare the Decree well ahead of time (see Chapter 7), and both parties sign their approval of it. Your property, if there is any, should be itemized in the Petition.

Read the rest of this book until you understand when and how the Decree is used, then prepare a Decree that is agreeable to both you and your spouse. Then, on the last page, in the lower left-hand corner, insert the following:

I approve of and consent to the above Decree.

Dated: ....
Respondent

I approve of the above Decree and agree to present it to the Court at the time of the hearing:

Dated: ....
Petitioner

Both parties date and sign the Decree. You will need the original and two copies to take to court and a signed copy for the Respondent to keep. Follow all the other instructions in this book, and when you get to the hearing, present the signed Decree to the judge. Tell the judge you recognize the signature as that of your spouse and that the Decree has been agreed to and approved by both of you. After the hearing, give the Respondent a certified copy of the Decree to show that the agreement was completed.

2. The Marital Settlement Contract

This kind of agreement is detailed and formal, and takes a bit of effort to work up. You should not make your own contract if you have a large or intricate estate, or if you have any confusion or uncertainty about it.

Every situation is different, and therefore every contract should be different. There is no one form that will do in every situation. The contract shown here is included so you can see what one looks like, how it goes. You can use it as a guide in preparing your own agreement. Use parts that apply to you and disregard others. Change it to suit your own case. Do not leave out paragraphs VIII, IX, X, or XI, however.

If you have any trouble at all understanding the contract or wording it to fit your situation, do not attempt to do it yourself. Get help (see Chapter A, section 12).

If you decide to make your own contract, make an original, a copy for your spouse, and three copies to take to the hearing with you. The contract has the same caption as the other forms because it gets filed and becomes an official court document. Mark one of the copies "Exhibit A" and attach it to your Decree so the agreement is properly before the Court.

Cause No._____

In the Matter of the Marriage of:

_____ Petitioner

and

_____ Respondent

And in the Interest of

_____

_____ Child(ren)

In the District Court

of _____ County

_____ Judicial District

Marital Settlement Contract

I, _____ , Husband,

and I, _____ , Wife, agree as follows:

I. GENERALLY: We are now husband and wife. We were married on   , 20   ,
and separated on   , 20   . We make this agreement with reference to the
following facts:

    A. Children: There are

        a) no children, and none are expected.

        b) the following minor children of the parties
            (*list by full name and give sex and birthdate for each child*).

    B. Our marriage has become insupportable because of discord or conflict of
       personalities such that there is no reasonable expectation for reconciliation.
       For this reason, we now desire to settle our mutual rights and duties as set
       forth below.

II. SEPARATION: We agree to live separately and apart, and, except for the duties and obligations imposed and assumed under this agreement, each shall be free from interference and control of the other as fully as if he or she were single. We each agree not to molest, interfere with, or harass the other.

III. CUSTODY OF CHILDREN: The (Wife/Husband) shall be the Managing Conservator of the child(ren), to have full parental rights, duties, and powers, subject only to the rights of the (Husband/Wife), as Possessory Conservator, to visit with and temporarily take possession of the child(ren) as follows: (*specify*)

(*see Chapter C, section 3 and the Schedule for Possession in Forms section*)

IV. SUPPORT OF CHILDREN: Subject to the power of the court to modify these terms, (Husband/Wife) shall pay to (Wife/Husband), as and for child support, the sum of $ per (wk./mo.), beginning on the   day of   , 20   , and continuing until the child reaches the age of 18, except that if the child is still in high school, the child support shall continue until the end of the school year in which the child graduates; the child marries; the child dies; the child is otherwise emancipated. Thereafter (Husband/Wife) shall pay to (Wife/Husband) as and for child support the sum of $ per (wk/mo.) beginning on the   (same day as above) of the first month following the occurrence of any of the above described events. (*If there is more than one child repeat the last sentence as many times as necessary until only one child is left to support.*)

This obligation shall survive the death of the obligor. This obligation shall cease if obligor becomes the Managing Conservator.

If there is a handicapped child, add this: Support for (*name of child*) shall continue beyond the age of eighteen, as said child requires continuous care and personal supervision and is unlikely to become self-supporting.

Optional terms:

In addition, during the term of the support obligation for the child(ren), (Husband/Wife) shall

a) carry and maintain life insurance in the amount of $ naming the child(ren) as beneficiary(ies).

b) carry and maintain medical and hospital insurance for the children's benefit.

c) pay for (required/extraordinary) medical and dental expenses.

V. PAYMENTS TO SPOUSE: In order to fully discharge all obligations arising from the marriage, other than division of property, (Husband/Wife) agrees to pay to (Wife/Husband) the sum of $_____ per month, payable on the _____ day of each month, beginning on _____, 20___, and continuing until:

   a) the death of (one) (either)

   b) the remarriage of the recipient

   c) some other date or condition

These spousal maintenance payments ___ may be ___ may not be the subject of an income withholding order.

VI. DIVISION OF PROPERTY AND DEBTS:

   A. Property Transferred to Wife: Husband transfers and quitclaims to Wife as her sole and separate property the following items: (*list — include items which are already Wife's separate property*).

   B. Property Transferred to Husband: Wife transfers and quitclaims to Husband as his sole and separate property the following items: (*list — include items that are already Husband's separate property*).

Note: If there is a community interest in a pension plan, be sure to list and dispose of it in this section.

Note: Here is an alternative way to deal with property for small estates: Husband and Wife agree that they have already divided the property to their mutual satisfaction, and each hereby transfers and quitclaims to the other any and all interest in any property in the possession of the other, and agrees that whatever property the other may possess is now the sole and separate property of the other.

   C. Insurance: Wife (or Husband) is expressly retained as the beneficiary of the following insurance policies: (*description*). —*or*— Wife (or Husband) is no longer the beneficiary of any insurance policy carried by Husband (or Wife).

   D. Debts Assumed by Husband: Husband shall pay and hold Wife harmless from the following debts: (*list and give specific description of each one*).

   E. Debts Assumed by Wife: Wife shall pay and hold Husband harmless from the following debts: (*list and give specific description of each one*).

VII. TAXES: The parties agree that:

Any tax refunds for the current tax year will be distributed as follows: (*specify*).

Any tax deficiencies for the current tax year shall be paid as follows: (*specify*).

VIII. EXECUTION OF INSTRUMENTS: Each party agrees to execute and deliver any documents, make all endorsements, and do all acts that are necessary or convenient to carry out the terms of this agreement.

IX. APPROVAL BY COURT: At the divorce proceeding, this agreement shall be presented to the court for incorporation into the Decree, and the parties shall, by the terms of the Decree, be ordered to comply with all terms of this agreement.

X. DISCLOSURES: Each party has made a full disclosure to the other of his or her current assets and income, and each enters into this agreement in reliance thereupon.

XI. BINDING EFFECT: This agreement, and each provision of it, is expressly made binding upon the heirs, assigns, executors, administrators, representatives and successors in interest of each party.

Dated: _____   _____
                                                    Husband

Dated: _____   _____
                                                    Wife

Part Two

How to Do Your Own Divorce

1. Introducing the Forms

In the back of this book you will find a complete set of forms for your use if you do your own divorce. An uncontested divorce requires only three to six legal forms and a Statistical Report. The legal forms you will use are these:

    a) the Petition

    b) either the Citation or the Waiver

    c) the Decree

Most cases with children will also use:

    d) the Order/Notice to Withhold Income for Child Support

    e) the Request to Issue Withholding Order

    f) the Schedule for Possession of Minor Children

The Petition states basic information about your marriage and tells the court what you want. When your spouse gets a copy of it, it will give notice of what you intend to ask for in court.

The Citation is a message from the court to your spouse commanding an answer to the Petition within 20 days. It also contains a form where the officer serving the papers signs the details of the service.

The Waiver is the statement of a cooperative spouse that the Petition was received and giving permission for the matter to proceed without contest.

The Order/Notice to Withhold Income for Child Support is used in almost every case where child support is ordered. When served on the paying spouse's employer it requires that sums be taken from wages and paid into an office of the court, then promptly remitted to the person caring for the children.

The Request to Issue Withholding Order is a simple request to the clerk to have the withholding order served on a specific, named employer so that it can go into effect.

The Schedule for Possession of Minor Children lists the detailed terms and conditions for possession (visitation) of the children.

The Decree contains the findings of fact and the orders of the court. It shows that your marriage was dissolved and gives the terms of the divorce.

2. Checklists

A. Preplanning Checklist

Once you have decided definitely to get a divorce, and after you have decided to do it yourself, you then have to plan out just how you are going to go about doing it:

1. Divorce by agreement or by default?

It is much easier and better if you can divorce by agreement, but much more common for it to be done by default. Carefully review Chapters A, section 5; A, section 9; and E. Try to work toward an agreed divorce, but if it cannot be done, or if you do not want to try it, proceed by default.

2. Decisions that must be made

    a) how to divide the property (Chapter B), *and*

    b) arrangements for child custody, visitation, and support (Chapters C and D).

3. Plan how to give notice to your spouse:

If you can proceed by agreement, you will undoubtedly have your spouse sign the Waiver form.

    If you proceed by default, you must consider how notice can be delivered to your spouse. If there is any chance that your spouse will try to evade service, you have to plan the best way to get through. See Chapter 6.

B. Checklist for the Agreed Divorce

1. Come to an agreement with your spouse about all aspects of the divorce. Actually divide up all the property. Settle matters concerning debts and children.

2. If you have children, real estate, a lot of property or the desire to be thorough and complete, then you should have a written agreement. Review Chapter E, decide whether to use the approved Decree or a contract, then prepare whichever you and your spouse decide to use.

3. Prepare the Petition (Chapter 5).

4. File the Petition (Chapter 4) and pay the filing fee with cash or a money order.

5. Prepare: the Waiver (Chapter 6, section A)
   the Decree (Chapter 7)
   the Info on Suit/Family Relationships (Chapter 9)

   If you request child support, you should also prepare:
   the Employer's Order to Withhold Earnings, and
   the Request to Issue Withholding Order (Chapter 8)

   Optional, but recommended when child support is requested:
   the Financial Information form (in back of book).

   If you have children, ask the Clerk if you and your spouse must attend a Helping Children Cope class (Chapter C, section 5), then prepare:
   the Schedule for Possession of Minor Children

6. Have your spouse sign the Waiver before a Notary Public. At this time your spouse should also sign any written agreement you have decided to use.

7. File the Waiver.

8. Choose a date and go to the Hearing (Chapter 10).

C. Checklist for the Default Divorce

1. Prepare the Petition (Chapter 5)

2. File the Petition (Chapter 4) and pay the filing fee with cash or a money order.

3. Arrange for the Citation to be served on your spouse. In a few counties you may have to prepare the Citation yourself (Chapter 6, section B).

4. Prepare: the Decree (Chapter 7)
   the Info on Suit/Family Relationships (Chapter 9)

   If you request child support, you should also prepare:
   the Employer's Order to Withhold Earnings, and
   the Request to Issue Withholding Order (Chapter 8)

   Optional, but recommended when child support is requested:
   the Financial Information form (in back of book).

   If you have children, ask the Clerk if you and your spouse must attend a Helping Children Cope class (Chapter C, section 5), then prepare:
   the Schedule for Possession of Minor Children

5. Choose a date and go to the Hearing (Chapter 10).

3. How to Use the Forms

The forms that come with this book are complete, legal, and they will work for you. In their present form, however, they suffer from one small disadvantage — they look different from forms attorneys present to the court. This is because they are made up to work for a lot of different cases instead of just yours. You have to cross out parts that you do not use. However, we repeat: they will work fine, they just look different.

There is no legal requirement that documents presented to a court be in any particular size, shape, or style. The only requirement stated in the law is that they be in writing, and even that rule has exceptions. However, there is a strong tradition attorneys almost universally follow. It is what judges are used to and what they expect to see. Legal forms, traditionally, are typed, double-spaced, on 8½ x 11-inch paper.

There is some advantage to having your papers look just like all the others the judge is used to seeing. Texans file over 90,000 divorces each year, so Texas judges are buried up to their ears in divorce cases. They do not have the time or desire to give special attention to any one of them if they can help it. Your case will get a little extra attention just because you are representing yourself. The judge may ask you some questions just to make sure that you know what you are doing. He or she may look a little more closely at the case to make sure it all checks out. This is why you have to be clear and sure about what you are doing. If any of your requests are unusual (giving custody of a child to a non-parent, or asking to change the husband's name to Florence, or taking $250 for support from a person who makes $100,000), then you are letting yourself in for some extra questions and explanations. It always goes much easier when your case is pretty much like all the others before and after it.

There are *two* ways you can use the forms in this book:

- **Custom-typed forms** can be made up by you or by a typist, using our forms as your guide. Copy our language and our format exactly, but leave out the parts that don't apply to your case. This will give you clean copy and your forms will look much like all the others on the judge's bench.

- **Computer forms** that you can word process yourself or fill out and print can be purchased on a floppy or downloaded from our website at www.nolotech.com.

- **Printed forms** that come with this book can be used. This is the easiest and cheapest thing for you to do, and, like we said, they will work just fine. If for any reason you want an extra set of blank forms, you can order them by using the order form in the back of this book.

A. General Instructions

These instructions show you how to use the forms that come with this book. Even if you decide to custom type your own set, or have it done for you by a typist, you should still make up one set of our forms as shown here and use them as your work sheets. It will help eliminate errors.

1. Keep all papers and receipts orderly, neat, and in one safe place.

2. Make high-quality copies of the blank forms so you will have extras in case you make a mistake.

3. The forms are designed so that if there are no children, entire pages can be pulled out and discarded.

4. On documents with more than one page, type in page numbers at the bottom center of each page, like this: "1 of 3," "2 of 3," "3 of 3." The last number is the total number of pages of that document, not including any attachments.

5. Use a typewriter to fill in the blanks in the forms as shown by the instructions. It is not illegal for you to hand print in ink, but the typewriter is much preferred.

6. Whatever parts are not used or do not apply to your case should be crossed out by drawing a heavy line through them in ink. Use a ruler to make straight lines.

7. When your forms are accurate and complete, make four high-quality copies of each one. You need only two, but it will be convenient to have more and it doesn't cost much.

B. The Caption

At the top of each legal document is a heading, called a caption, which is filled out like this:

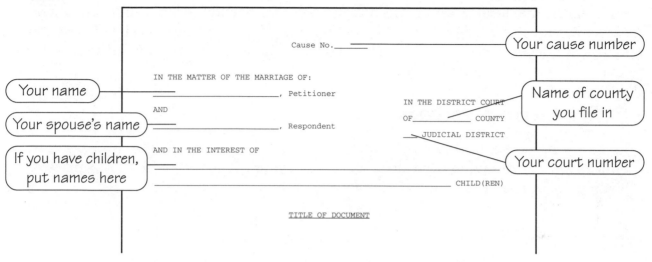

The Cause Number (case number) and the Judicial District Number (number of your court) are assigned when you file the Petition, and after that must be filled in on any document you file. The Court Number identifies your court, the one that will be handling and hearing your case. The Cause Number is their identification for your file and case.

If there are children of this marriage, they must be named in the caption; otherwise that part of the caption is crossed out, or left off. Include any legally adopted children. If the wife is pregnant, do not start your own divorce until the child is born.

C. Petitioner/Respondent

In case you haven't figured it out yet, the Petitioner is the spouse that files the papers and goes to court. The Respondent is the other spouse. Apart from possibly signing a Waiver and/or written agreement, the Respondent does nothing — files no papers, does not go to court.

D. Pro Se

This term appears in a few places on the forms and you may hear it in court. It is a legal Latin term meaning "for self," which indicates that you are appearing as your own attorney.

E. Names

Use the full legal names of parties and children. You must be consistent, so names will appear exactly the same way each time, including signatures. The court will not know, for instance, that John Smith, J. W. Smith, John W. Smith, and J. Wilson Smith are different names for the same person. It is good form to type the names in capitals. Use the names in normal order — last names go last. Use the wife's married name unless the form requests her maiden name.

F. Protecting Privacy

In cases where you need or want to protect the location of a party or a child, you can omit any of the following from all papers filed in your divorce: the child's sex, place of birth, place of residence, and the parents' ages and places of residence.

G. Copies

Type each form neatly, check for errors, then make four copies of each page on a high-quality copy machine. When there is more than one page to a document, staple the pages together in the upper left-hand corner.

The court always gets the original of each form, the Respondent gets a copy, and you keep a copy for your files. Thus you need an original and two copies of each document, but you should make two extra copies in case you want them later. It is an especially good idea to have extra copies of the Decree. When you file the Decree, have the clerk certify your copies, and keep them for future use.

4. How to File Your Papers

Filing papers is easy. All you do is take them down to the District Clerk's Office and hand them to the clerk. When you file the Petition, you must also pay the filing fee.

The county in which you file your papers is determined by the residency requirements (Chapter A, section 8) and is usually the one you live in. Papers are filed at the District Clerk's Office in that county. Get the address of the District Clerk's Office by calling them on the telephone. The number will be listed under the name of your county, or under "Government" in the phone book. Do not confuse them with the County Clerk's Office, which is a different thing altogether.

When you file your Petition, the clerk will give you your Cause Number and assign your case to a court by filling in the number of the Judicial District in your Caption. From this time on, all documents filed in your case must have these numbers on them.

Fees: When you have the District Clerk's Office on the phone, ask them how much the filing fee will be for your case. The fees vary slightly from county to county, and depend mostly on whether there is a Waiver, an in-county Citation, or an out-of-county Citation. Describe your case. Tell them you want to know the filing fee for a Divorce Petition, (with/without) children, and an (in-county/out-of-county) Citation.

Fees must be paid by cash, money order, or cashier's check made payable to "District Clerk, (name of county), Texas." Be sure to get a receipt and keep it in your file. *If you can't afford the fees,* you can file a Pauper's Oath — a sworn statement about your financial inability — and the fees will be waived. There is a blank Pauper's Oath form in the Appendix section of this book.

If your case will not have a Waiver signed by the Respondent, then a Citation will have to be prepared, issued by the clerk, and forwarded to an officer for service. In most counties, the District Clerk's Office does this for you on their own forms, but some do not. When you have the clerk on the phone, ask whether or not they prepare the Citation, or if it is prepared by the Petitioner. Ask if they forward the Citation for service.

The clerks will not be willing to give you legal advice because they are not attorneys and it would be against the law for them to do so. But if they wish to, they can be very helpful with matters pertaining to the filing of papers and how procedures are handled in their office. Don't be afraid to ask questions. You should also remember that most employees of the District Clerk's offices are (or feel they are) overworked and underpaid. A big smile and politeness on your part can go a long way toward getting your questions answered.

4. How to File Your Papers

5. The Petition

What it is:

The Petition states basic information about your marriage, and tells the court what you want done. When it is served on the Respondent, it gives notice of what is happening in court. If the Respondent declines to respond, then the judge is free to assume that all the facts stated in it are true, and the Petitioner's requests are very likely to be granted.

How to fill it out:

Fill out the Petition as shown in the illustrations on the next pages.

Then what?

When the forms are completed, check them for accuracy. Make four copies on a high-quality copy machine, then take the original and all four copies to the District Clerk's Office along with the filing fee (use a money order). The clerk will assign a Cause number and Court number at this time. If you are using the Citation and service method to give notice to your spouse, then take along whatever papers you need for this purpose (see Chapter 6).

Notes for the first page

Note 1. In the caption, the Cause Number and the Court Number are left blank. They are assigned by the clerk when you file the Petition. We are told that some counties word this block a little differently—such as *COUNTY COURT AT LAW, NO. ____*. Call your County Clerk to ask how they want this caption worded.

Note 2. Children and the Caption: If you have children, you must name them in the caption, but remember that you should include only children born to or adopted by you and your spouse. Do not include stepchildren who have not been legally adopted by the stepparent. If the wife is pregnant, do not do your own divorce until the child is born.

Note 3. Give the Respondent's complete street address, not just a post office box.

Note 4. As the **first** sentence of your Petition, immediately after the title "ORIGINAL PETITION FOR DIVORCE," type in **one** of the following sentences:

A. Use this sentence if a) there are **no** minor children of the marriage whose custody and support will be determined **and** b) the value of the marital estate (marital assets minus marital debt) is between zero and $50,000.00.

Discovery Level 1 applies to this case as there are no minor children of the marriage whose custody and support will be determined AND the value of the marital estate is between zero and $50,000.00.

B. For all other cases, use this sentence.

Discovery Level 2 applies to this case as there are minor children of the marriage whose custody and support will be determined AND/OR the value of the marital estate is more than $50,000.00

Note 5: Privacy. In cases where you need to protect the location of a party or a child, you can omit any of the following from all papers filed in your divorce: the child's sex, place of birth, place of residence; and the parents' ages and places of residence.

How to fill out the Petition

First page

Cause No._____

Leave blank

IN THE MATTER OF THE MARRIAGE OF:

Your name

_____, Petitioner

AND

Your spouse's name

_____, Respondent

IN THE DISTRICT COURT

OF _____ COUNTY

_____ JUDICIAL DISTRICT

Name of the county you file in

Leave blank

AND IN THE INTEREST OF

_____

_____ CHILD(REN)

If you have children, put names here, otherwise cross this part out

ORIGINAL PETITION FOR DIVORCE

/...Discovery Level 1 applies to this case as there are no minor children of the marriage whose custody and support will be determined AND the value of the marital estate is between zero and $50,000.00.

...Discovery Level 2 applies to this case as there are minor children of the marriage whose custody and support will be determined AND/OR the value of the marital estate is more than $50,000.00.

Choose one. See Note 4 on previous page.

This suit is brought by _____

Petitioner, Soc. Sec.#_____, Driver's License #_____

age_____, who resides at

_____

Your name, social security and driver's license numbers, age and address. See Note 5.

Respondent is _____

Soc.Sec.# _____, Driver's License #_____ age_____,

who resides at _____

Your spouse's name, social security and driver's license numbers, age and address.

I. RESIDENCY:

Petitioner has been a domiciliary of the State of Texas for the preceding six months and a resident of the county in which this petition is filed for the preceding ninety days.

....Respondent is a domiciliary of the State of Texas.

....Long Arm: Respondent is a nonresident of Texas.

Cross out statement that is not true

Page 1 of __

Put in total number of pages in Petition

Notes for the second page

Note 1: Service of Process. If papers are to be served on the Respondent, then give a complete residence address, and also add the employment address if you know it.

Note 2: Common-Law Marriage. Remember, you must file for divorce within two years of separation if your marriage is a common-law one rather than ceremonial. If you wait longer than that, it is presumed that the marriage never existed and you can't go through a regular divorce. In cases like this you will have to find another way to establish paternity of any children born during the relationship in order to collect support and arrange for visitation.

Note 3: Property. Review Chapter B carefully, especially sections 2, 4, and 5. If you and your spouse are in agreement but have not worked out the details, you may use the second paragraph and cross out the other paragraphs. If you have property which will not be divided by a written agreement, then you must use the fourth paragraph under item V (cross the other three out). Itemize your property on page three of the Decree as shown below. If there is not enough room in the Decree for your entire list, then do not put any of it on the form. Instead, just type in these words:

> "As listed on attached sheet entitled 'Property List,'
> which is incorporated here by reference."

Then, on a blank sheet, type the heading "Property List" and make your list as shown below. Staple it to the Petition.

Number each item or group of items. It is best, though not required, to give the approximate market values (what you could get if you tried to sell at this time).

You should *list separately:*

- any item that has special importance to you,
- any property with documentary title (real estate, bank accounts, vehicles, pension plans, insurance policies with cash surrender value, stocks, etc),
- property that is encumbered by debt, together with to whom owed, amount due, and repayment schedule.

All other property can be grouped under general headings.

Examples for how to list property is on the next page.

How to fill out the Petition

Second page

Cross out parts that do not apply to your case

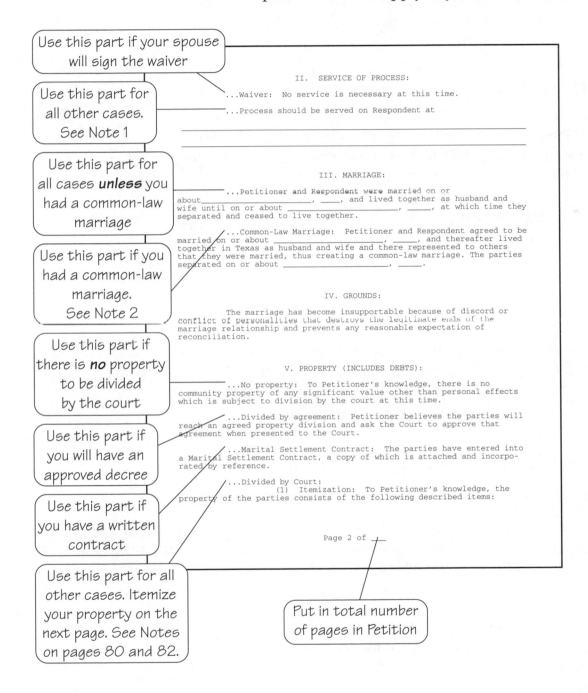

Use this part if your spouse will sign the waiver

Use this part for all other cases. See Note 1

Use this part for all cases **unless** you had a common-law marriage

Use this part if you had a common-law marriage. See Note 2

Use this part if there is **no** property to be divided by the court

Use this part if you will have an approved decree

Use this part if you have a written contract

Use this part for all other cases. Itemize your property on the next page. See Notes on pages 80 and 82.

Put in total number of pages in Petition

II.   SERVICE OF PROCESS:

...Waiver: No service is necessary at this time.

...Process should be served on Respondent at

III. MARRIAGE:

...Petitioner and Respondent were married on or about_____, _____, and lived together as husband and wife until on or about _____, _____, at which time they separated and ceased to live together.

...Common-Law Marriage: Petitioner and Respondent agreed to be married on or about _____, and thereafter lived together in Texas as husband and wife and there represented to others that they were married, thus creating a common-law marriage. The parties separated on or about _____, _____.

IV. GROUNDS:

The marriage has become insupportable because of discord or conflict of personalities that destroys the legitimate ends of the marriage relationship and prevents any reasonable expectation of reconciliation.

V. PROPERTY (INCLUDES DEBTS):

...No property: To Petitioner's knowledge, there is no community property of any significant value other than personal effects which is subject to division by the court at this time.

...Divided by agreement: Petitioner believes the parties will reach an agreed property division and ask the Court to approve that agreement when presented to the Court.

...Marital Settlement Contract: The parties have entered into a Marital Settlement Contract, a copy of which is attached and incorporated by reference.

...Divided by Court:
     (1) Itemization: To Petitioner's knowledge, the property of the parties consists of the following described items:

Page 2 of ___

Notes for the third page

Note 1: Marital Property. There are many ways you could list your marital property, but we suggest you do it something like this:

1. Personal effects of the Petitioner $465

    Personal effects of the Respondent 875
    (covers clothing, ordinary jewelry, hair brushes, etc.)

2. Sable stole.. 650

3. Household goods, furnishings, appliances 1200

4. Sony 19" remote control color T.V 350

5. 1958 Edsel, license no. HOG 101, vehicle I.D. no. 24564R556,
    encumbered by debt to Good Guy Finance Co. in amount
    of $853, payable $75 per month 1400

6. The Respondent's vested retirement account, Teacher's Union
    Retirement Account no. 76R456 8000

7. House and lot located at 10 Downing Street, Clyde, Texas, described
    as Lot 1, Section 3, on Map 33, Page 4, Plat Records, Cork County,
    Texas, encumbered by Loan no. 54-56-78900, Lubbock First National
    Bank, Lubbock, Texas in the amount of approximately $33,654,
    payable at $144 per month 40500

Note 2: Separate Property. Items of any value or importance to you that you claim to be yours separately should be specifically listed and valued. Type in a heading and list items under it like this:

Petitioner's separate property:

8. Family heirloom gold chain $1200

9. Oil paintings of a seascape and a cucumber 45

Do the same for Respondent's separate property, if there is any.

Note 3: Debts. Any debt not already listed as secured by some property item should be listed separately, together with a word or two about what it's for, the amount, payment schedule, and to whom owed. For example:

Debts:

10. Home Finance Co., for dental work, $75 per month $839

11. J. Jones, Respondent's father, for vacation, no fixed
    schedule of payments 950

Notice that the item numbers run consecutively through the entire list.

More notes for the third page

If you claimed no property (by using the first paragraph under item V on page 2) or if you indicated a written agreement (by using the second paragraph under item V) then you do **not** use item (2) on this page. Cross it out.

If you **do** use item (2), the judge will inquire about your property and make orders dividing it (unless you show up in court with a written agreement). The paragraphs under item (2) are alternative requests from you to the court stating how you wish to have the property divided. It is not required that you use any of the alternative paragraphs under item (2); you **could** cross them all out, thus leaving the entire matter up to the court to decide. However, judges greatly prefer it if you indicate ahead of time the way you would like the property and debts to be divided. It makes their job, and yours, much easier at the hearing.

Notes for the fourth page

Note 1: If you do not want maintenance (alimony) or if you have already arranged for it in a Marital Settlement Contract, cross out everything after the first sentence. If you request alimony, choose whether you are asking for alimony based on a ten-year marriage or on a family violence occurrence or both. Then choose which of the three additional grounds apply and cross out the others.

Note 2: Privacy. In cases where you need to protect the location of a party or a child, you can omit any of the following from all papers filed in your divorce: the child's sex, place of birth, place of residence; and the parents' ages and places of residence.

Note 3: Children. If there are no children from this marriage (either born to you both or adopted), use the first sentence and cross out the rest of section VIII.

How to fill out the Petition

Third page

Cross out parts that do not apply to your case

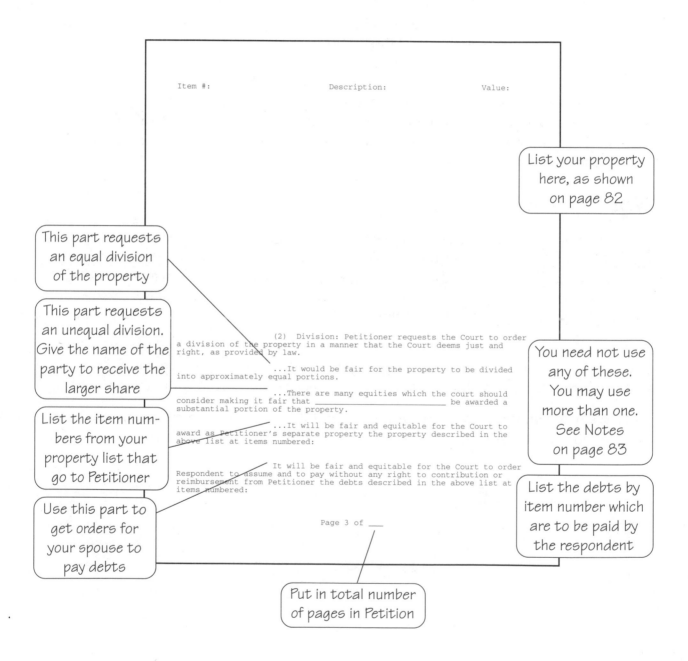

Item #:   Description: Value:

List your property here, as shown on page 82

This part requests an equal division of the property

This part requests an unequal division. Give the name of the party to receive the larger share

List the item numbers from your property list that go to Petitioner

Use this part to get orders for your spouse to pay debts

(2) Division: Petitioner requests the Court to order a division of the property in a manner that the Court deems just and right, as provided by law.

...It would be fair for the property to be divided into approximately equal portions.

...There are many equities which the court should consider making it fair that _____ be awarded a substantial portion of the property.

...It will be fair and equitable for the Court to award as Petitioner's separate property the property described in the above list at items numbered:

It will be fair and equitable for the Court to order Respondent to assume and to pay without any right to contribution or reimbursement from Petitioner the debts described in the above list at items numbered:

Page 3 of ____

You need not use any of these. You may use more than one. See Notes on page 83

List the debts by item number which are to be paid by the respondent

Put in total number of pages in Petition

How to fill out the Petition

Fourth page

Cross out parts that do not apply to your case

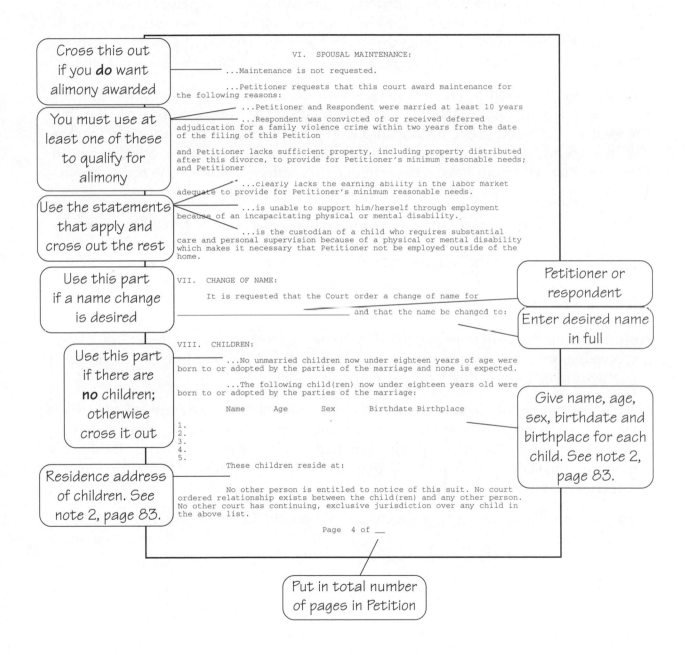

Cross this out if you **do** want alimony awarded

You must use at least one of these to qualify for alimony

Use the statements that apply and cross out the rest

Use this part if a name change is desired

Use this part if there are **no** children; otherwise cross it out

Residence address of children. See note 2, page 83.

Petitioner or respondent

Enter desired name in full

Give name, age, sex, birthdate and birthplace for each child. See note 2, page 83.

Put in total number of pages in Petition

VI. SPOUSAL MAINTENANCE:

...Maintenance is not requested.

...Petitioner requests that this court award maintenance for the following reasons:

...Petitioner and Respondent were married at least 10 years
...Respondent was convicted of or received deferred adjudication for a family violence crime within two years from the date of the filing of this Petition

and Petitioner lacks sufficient property, including property distributed after this divorce, to provide for Petitioner's minimum reasonable needs; and Petitioner

...clearly lacks the earning ability in the labor market adequate to provide for Petitioner's minimum reasonable needs.

...is unable to support him/herself through employment because of an incapacitating physical or mental disability.

...is the custodian of a child who requires substantial care and personal supervision because of a physical or mental disability which makes it necessary that Petitioner not be employed outside of the home.

VII. CHANGE OF NAME:

It is requested that the Court order a change of name for

_____ and that the name be changed to:

VIII. CHILDREN:

...No unmarried children now under eighteen years of age were born to or adopted by the parties of the marriage and none is expected.

...The following child(ren) now under eighteen years old were born to or adopted by the parties of the marriage:

Name   Age   Sex   Birthdate Birthplace

1.
2.
3.
4.
5.

These children reside at:

No other person is entitled to notice of this suit. No court ordered relationship exists between the child(ren) and any other person. No other court has continuing, exclusive jurisdiction over any child in the above list.

Page 4 of __

Notes for the fifth page

Note 1: Health insurance. The court needs to know whether or not private health insurance is in effect and, if it is, the name of the insurance company, the policy number, the amount of the premium and whether Petitioner or Respondent is paying it, and whether coverage is provided through employment. If no private health insurance is in effect, indicate whether the child is receiving health care under any public assistance program (name the program) and whether private health insurance is available at reasonable cost to either parent. Reasonable cost = 10% of obligor's net income.

Note 2: Conservatorship. The Texas Legislature decided that it is best for the children if the parents have Joint Managing Conservatorship. The hope is to provide the children with a stable, on-going relationship with both parents. It does *not* mean that the children spend half their time with you and half their time with the other parent. It *does* mean that you both have a voice in decisions affecting them. The rights and responsibilities of both parents are spelled out in detail in your Decree.

If there are reasons why you think Joint Managing Conservatorship will not work for your children (see Chapter C), then take the second option under Paragraph IX, but be prepared to explain to the Judge what those reasons are.

Notes for the sixth page

Note 1. Most judges are now interested in domestic violence issues. If you don't have a protective order in effect or pending, cross out all but the first line. If you do have one, it would be best to attach copies if at all possible.

Note 2. The statement about alternative dispute resolution is an attempt to keep issues about child custody and support from having to be fought out in court, but you wouldn't be doing your own divorce if you had that problem, would you? If they ask you to sign the statement, don't hesitate to do so, even though your signature is just a few inches down the paper already.

Note 3. If your spouse is signing a waiver, cross out the first line under "PRAYER."

How to fill out the Petition

Fifth page

Cross out parts that do not apply to your case

If any child owns property other than personal effects list it here; otherwise type "none"

Use this part if you have a handicapped child; give name of child

If children have health insurance, enter party who pays for it, and amount paid.

If kids have no health insurance, use the statement that applies.

Use this if you want JMC. Enter Petitioner or Respondent to show who establishes primary residence

Use this if you do not want JMC and enter Petitioner and Respondent for MC and PC

If Respondent is not a resident of Texas you must use at least one of these; cross out items that are not true

Enter name of insurance company and policy number.

If kids have public health care, give name of program(s).

Enter Petitioner or Respondent. If JMC, it is the parent who does not establish primary residence. In MC/PC, it is the PC parent

Put in total number of pages in Petition

No property, apart from personal effects, is owned by the child(ren) in the above list, except as listed here:

..._____, a child of this marriage, requires continuous care and personal supervision because of a disability and will not be capable of self-support. The Court is requested to order that payments for the support of this child be continued after the child's eighteenth birthday and extended for an indefinite period.

...Respondent is not a resident of Texas, but this court may exercise personal jurisdiction over him because:

...The above child(ren) (was/were) conceived in Texas and Respondent is a parent.

...Respondent resided in Texas and provided prenatal expenses and/or support for the child(ren).

...Respondent resided with the child(ren) in Texas

...The child(ren) reside(s) in Texas as a result of the acts or directives or with the approval of the Respondent.

...Private health care coverage is currently in effect for the child(ren) and _____ is responsible for paying the premium of _____ per month. Said insurance, (provided / not provided) through the payor's employment, is via the following policy:

...There is currently no private health care coverage in effect for the child(ren) and

...the child(ren) is/are not receiving health care under any public health care program.

...the child(ren) is/are receiving health care under the following public health care program(s): _____

IX.   CONSERVATORSHIP AND SUPPORT:

Upon final hearing,

...Petitioner and Respondent should be appointed Joint Managing Conservators of the child(ren) and _____ should have the right to establish the primary residence of the child(ren).

..._____ should be appointed the Sole Managing Conservator of the child(ren) and _____ should be appointed Possessory Conservator of the child(ren).

_____ should be ordered to make payments for the support of the children in the manner specified by the Court. Possession should be arranged according to the best interests of the child(ren).

Page 5 of ____

How to fill out the Petition

Sixth page

Cross out parts that do not apply to your case

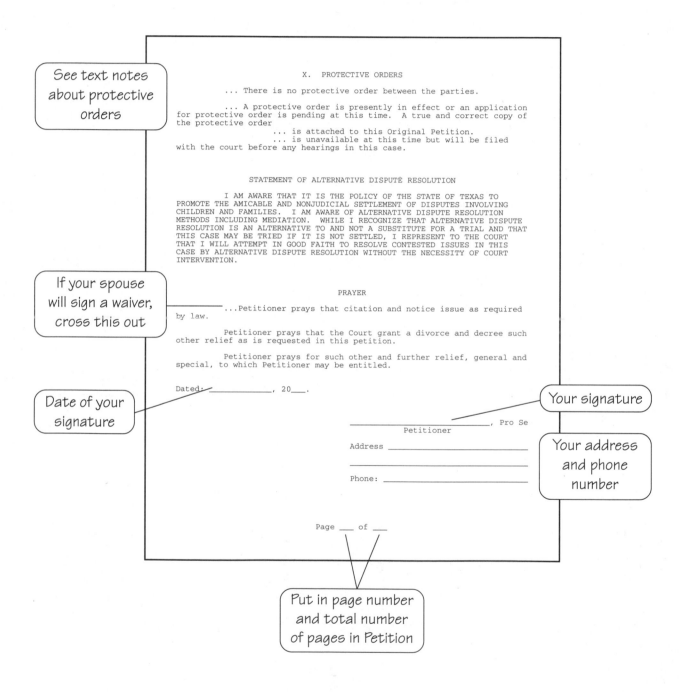

See text notes about protective orders

X. PROTECTIVE ORDERS

... There is no protective order between the parties.

... A protective order is presently in effect or an application for protective order is pending at this time. A true and correct copy of the protective order
... is attached to this Original Petition.
... is unavailable at this time but will be filed with the court before any hearings in this case.

STATEMENT OF ALTERNATIVE DISPUTE RESOLUTION

I AM AWARE THAT IT IS THE POLICY OF THE STATE OF TEXAS TO PROMOTE THE AMICABLE AND NONJUDICIAL SETTLEMENT OF DISPUTES INVOLVING CHILDREN AND FAMILIES. I AM AWARE OF ALTERNATIVE DISPUTE RESOLUTION METHODS INCLUDING MEDIATION. WHILE I RECOGNIZE THAT ALTERNATIVE DISPUTE RESOLUTION IS AN ALTERNATIVE TO AND NOT A SUBSTITUTE FOR A TRIAL AND THAT THIS CASE MAY BE TRIED IF IT IS NOT SETTLED, I REPRESENT TO THE COURT THAT I WILL ATTEMPT IN GOOD FAITH TO RESOLVE CONTESTED ISSUES IN THIS CASE BY ALTERNATIVE DISPUTE RESOLUTION WITHOUT THE NECESSITY OF COURT INTERVENTION.

If your spouse will sign a waiver, cross this out

PRAYER

...Petitioner prays that citation and notice issue as required by law.

Petitioner prays that the Court grant a divorce and decree such other relief as is requested in this petition.

Petitioner prays for such other and further relief, general and special, to which Petitioner may be entitled.

Dated: _____, 20___.

Date of your signature

Your signature

_____, Pro Se
Petitioner

Address _____
_____
Phone: _____

Your address and phone number

Page ___ of ___

Put in page number and total number of pages in Petition

6. Notice to Your Spouse

Proper notice to the Respondent is fundamental to the power of the court to act in your case. Chapter A, section 9 explains why this is so, and here we show you how it is done.

When you appear at the hearing, it *must* appear in the court's file that notice was properly accomplished. This can be shown by:

1. The Respondent's signed Waiver, *or*

2. The Citation, signed and returned by an officer, stating that he or she personally served papers on the Respondent.

Note: If your spouse is on active military duty, then the waiver is the *only* way you can proceed without an attorney.

Using the Waiver is the easiest method because you do not need to have the Citation issued and papers served. It helps to smooth the way at the hearing, because the judge can see that your spouse is in the picture and more or less agreeable to the divorce. Filing the Waiver is free.

If it is clear that your spouse will not go before a Notary Public and sign the Waiver, then don't waste your time with it. But if there is any chance, then at least give it a try. Be creative — talk nice, write a letter or have a mutual friend take the Waiver over and explain things. If your spouse still won't sign it and is *not* on active military duty, you can always have papers served by Citation.

If your spouse will not sign a Waiver, and successfully evades service, you will have to get help from an attorney. If you have no idea where your spouse is, you will have to do Citation by "Publication" or "Posting." See Chapter A, section 9.

A. The Waiver

What it is

The Waiver is a sworn document, signed by your spouse before a Notary Public, which states that the Petition was received and that the case can proceed without further notice. It is, in effect, a consent to an uncontested divorce.

How to fill it out

Fill out the first page as shown in the illustration. The second page (not shown) is where the Respondent signs before a Notary Public.

Then what?

1. Check it over, then make three copies.

2. Send your spouse:

    - the original and one copy of the Waiver, *and*

    - one copy of the Petition. Your spouse *must* get a copy of the Petition.

3. *Do not* allow the Waiver to be signed before the Petition is filed. File the Petition first, then give the Waiver to your spouse. If the Waiver is dated before the Petition is filed, then it is not valid, no good, void.

4. Tell your spouse that the Waiver *must* be signed before a Notary Public. The *original*, signed and notarized, is to be returned to you as soon as possible.

5. If your spouse is also going to approve the Decree as described in Chapter E, then this is the best time to do it. Prepare the Decree as shown in Chapter 7, send the original and one copy along with the other papers, and make sure the original Decree is returned to you after it is signed on the last page. If you are using the Decree form straight out of this book, and if any parts of it are crossed out, then your spouse should initial each and every cross-out in the margin.

6. Take the original, signed and sworn Waiver down to the District Clerk's Office and file it.

How to fill out the Waiver

First page

Put in your cause number

Fill out the caption as shown for Petition

This part is filled out by the Notary

Your spouse's name

Your spouse's name, social security and driver's license numbers and address

Cause No _____

IN THE MATTER OF THE MARRIAGE OF:

_____, Petitioner

AND

_____, Respondent

AND IN THE INTEREST OF

_____

_____CHILD(REN)

IN THE DISTRICT COURT

OF _____COUNTY

___ JUDICIAL DISTRICT

WAIVER OF CITATION

THE STATE OF _____

COUNTY OF _____

     BEFORE ME, the undersigned authority, on this day personally appeared _____ who, being by me duly sworn, upon oath says:

     My name is _____
Social Security #_____ Driver's License #_____
My address is _____
_____

     I am the Respondent in the above entitled and numbered cause. I have received a copy of the Original Petition which I have read and understand.

     I hereby enter my appearance in said cause for all purposes, waive the issuance, service and return of citation upon me, and agree that said cause may be taken up and considered by the Court at any time without further notice to me. I agree that this case may be heard by a duly appointed master or referee of this court. I waive the making of a record of testimony.

Page 1 of 2

B. The Citation

What it is

The Citation is a communication from the court to the Respondent giving notice of the Petition and ordering an answer in writing within about 20 days. Unless you plan to use a Waiver, have the clerk issue the Citation when you file your Petition. To be effective it must be properly served on the Respondent (see below).

There are two different Citation forms, one used if your spouse lives in the same county as you, and the other for out-of-county service. The only difference is in the Return portion, which is signed off by the serving officer. An out-of-county Return **must** be signed before a Notary Public.

How to fill it out

The Citation is prepared by the clerk in most Texas counties, but in a few counties the Petitioner must prepare the document and present it with the Petition at the time of filing. Call the clerk's office and ask who is responsible for preparing it in your county. It's easy, either way. If the clerk prepares the Citation, it will probably be mailed out, either to you or to the serving officer.

We have included two Citation forms in this book, one for in-county and one for out-of-county service, just in case you have need of one. Fill out the one you need as shown in the illustrations. Check it over, then make three copies.

Then what? Service of papers on Respondent

The Citation, after it is issued by the clerk, must be forwarded to an officer for personal service on your spouse. You get to choose whether the Sheriff or the Constable will serve your papers. We recommend that you use the Sheriff. In many counties the court also has a list of private process servers you can use. They are usually faster than public officers. If you are in a hurry to get the papers served, ask the clerk if they have such a list. You might be referred to a court coordinator for the list.

If service is made in the same county, then some clerks collect the fee for service with the filing fee and forward the papers for you. In other counties you will have to do it yourself. In all cases where service is to be made in another county, you will have to forward the papers and fee yourself. It's easy; just call the Sheriff in the county where Respondent can be found, tell them where Respondent is located and ask for the correct fee and for an address to send the papers to.

It is not required, but we strongly recommend that you send an information sheet along with the Citation, giving as much information as you have about the Respondent's whereabouts and habits, together with a complete description and, if possible, a recent and clear photograph. A form is provided in this book for you to use.

Inside the county, the serving officer has a choice of two methods for getting the papers to your spouse: they can be personally carried out and handed over, or they can be mailed by registered or certified mail, delivery restricted to addressee only. Knowing your spouse as well as you do (don't you?), if you have the idea that one method or the other is more likely to succeed, then include that on your information sheet.

The Citation *must* be served within 90 days of the date of issuance, or else returned unserved. If, by error, it is served after the 90 days, it will be defective and will not support a valid judgment. If your spouse is not served within the 90 days, then you will either have to have a new Citation issued and forwarded for service all over again (a new try, in other words) or you will have to get help from an attorney.

Hard Cases: First of all, do not have the Citation issued until you have a good idea where the Respondent can be found. You do not want to waste part of your 90 days just trying to locate your spouse. If you think the Respondent may try to avoid service, you should certainly indicate this on your information sheet, together with any ideas you have as to how service can best be accomplished.

If, during the 90 days, you get better information as to how the Respondent may be found and served, then don't delay getting this information to the serving officer. If it is near the end of the 90-day period when you get a hot lead, then it is best to have a new Citation issued.

The serving officer is unlikely to do anything very creative about finding and serving your spouse. It is *your* responsibility to give the best and most complete information you can about how to locate and identify your spouse. Dig hard. Talk to people; write, call, be a detective. Make your information sheet very complete, clear, and specific.

Citation and Service of Process Checklist

1. File the Petition

- take in your information sheet,

- take in the Citation, too, in those counties where the clerk does not make it up for you, and

- tell the clerk that you want the Sheriff to serve the papers.

2. Forward the papers to the Sheriff

Forward them to the Sheriff of the county where the Respondent is to be served. Where service is to be in your own county, the clerk may do this, but in cases where you do it and not the clerk, then:

- call the Sheriff's office and ask how much the service will cost.

- send the original Citation, the information sheet, and a copy of the Petition, include a money order for the fees charged by the Sheriff.

- tell the out-of-county Sheriff that the return must be sworn before a Notary Public according to Texas law.

3. Return of Citation

- It will be returned blank if service was not made. It will be filled out and signed if service was successful.

- If forwarded to the Sheriff by the clerk it will come back to the clerk, with notice by post card to you. You should go down to the clerk's office to make sure it is really on file, accurately filled out and signed by the officer.

- If forwarded by you, it will come back to you. You should check the return over and quickly get it on file at the District Clerk's Office.

- If service was not made, communicate with the Sheriff to find out what the problem was. You can either send out a new Citation and try one more time to get the Respondent served, or you can refer the case to an attorney for help.

How to fill out the Citation

For service within the County

THE STATE OF TEXAS   (Respondent Within the County)

Notice to Defendant: You have been sued. You may employ an attorney. If you or your attorney do not file a written answer with the clerk who issued this citation by 10:00 a.m. on the Monday next following the expiration of twenty days after you were served this citation and petition, a default judgment may be taken against you.

TO: _____ Defendant, Greeting:

You are hereby commanded to appear by filing a written answer to the Plaintiff's Petition at or before ten o'clock a.m. of the Monday next after the expiration of twenty days after the date of service of this citation before the ____ District Court of _____ County, Texas, at the courthouse of said County in the City of _____ , Texas.

Said Plaintiff's Petition was filed in said court on the ____ day of _____, 20___, in this case, numbered _____, and styled

_____, Petitioner, and _____, Respondent.

The nature of Petitioner's demand is fully shown by a true and correct copy of the Petition accompanying this citation and made a part hereof.

The officer executing this writ shall promptly serve the same according to requirements of law, and the mandates thereof, and make due return as the law directs. Issued and given under my hand and seal of said Court at _____, Texas, this the _____ day of _____, 20___.

Attest: _____
Clerk, District Court, _____ County, Texas
By _____ , Deputy.

OFFICER'S RETURN

The within citation came to hand on the ____ day of _____, 20___, at _____ o'clock (am)(pm), and was by me executed at _____, within the county of _____ , at _____ o'clock (am)(pm), on the _____ day of _____, 20___, by delivering to the within named _____ in person, a true copy of this citation, having first endorsed thereon the date of delivery, together with the accompanying true and correct copy of the Petition.

Sheriff's Fee....................... $_____

Sheriff Account

No. _____

To certify which witness my hand officially: _____

Sheriff of _____ County, Texas
By _____ , Deputy

For Clerk's Use
Taxed _____
Return recorded _____

Number and county of your court

Your cause number

Your name

Your spouse's name

City where your court sits

Date Petition was filed

Your spouse's name

Clerk fills out this part

The rest is filled out by officer serving papers

How to fill out the Citation

For service outside the County

Number and county of your court

Your cause number

Your name

Clerk fills out this part

The rest is filled out by officer serving papers

Your spouse's name

City where your court sits

Date Petition was filed

Your spouse's name

THE STATE OF TEXAS   (Respondent Without the County)

Notice to Defendant: You have been sued. You may employ an attorney. If you or your attorney do not file a written answer with the clerk who issued this citation by 10:00 a.m. on the Monday next following the expiration of twenty days after you were served this citation and petition, a default judgment may be taken against you.

TO: _____ Defendant, Greeting:

You are hereby commanded to appear by filing a written answer to the Plaintiff's Petition at or before ten o'clock a.m. of the Monday next after the expiration of twenty days after the date of service of this citation before the ___ District Court of _____ County, Texas, at the courthouse of said County in the City of _____,Texas.

Said Plaintiff's Petition was filed in said court on the ____ day of _____, 20___, in this case, numbered _____, and styled

_____, Petitioner, and _____, Respondent.

The nature of Petitioner's demand is fully shown by a true and correct copy of the Petition accompanying this citation and made a part hereof.

The officer executing this writ shall promptly serve the same according to requirements of law, and the mandates thereof, and make due return as the law directs. Issued and given under my hand and seal of said Court at _____, Texas, this the _____ day of _____, 20___.

Attest: _____
Clerk, District Court, _____ County, Texas
By _____ , Deputy.

RETURN

The State of _____
County of _____

Before me, the undersigned authority, on this day personally appeared _____ _____,a person not interested in the within-mentioned suit, above 21 years of age, of sound mind and competent to make oath, and being sworn, deposed and said:

My name is _____ ; I am disinterested in the within styled and numbered cause, above 21 years of age, of sound mind and competent to make oath of the facts below:

The within citation came to hand on the ____ day of _____, 20___ at _____ o'clock (am)(pm), and was by me executed at _____, within the county of _____ at _____ o'clock (am)(pm), on the _____ day of _____, 20___, by delivering to the within named _____ in person, a true copy of this citation, having first endorsed thereon the date of delivery, together with the accompanying true and correct copy of the Petition.

The distance actualy travelled by me in serving such process was _____ miles, and my fees are as follows: For serving this citation .... $ _____
    For mileage .... $ _____
    For notary .... $ _____
        Total fees .... $ _____

Sheriff Account

No. _____

To certify which witness my hand officially
Signed and sworn to by the said _____ , before me this _____ day of _____, 20___ to certify which witness my hand and seal of office.

For Clerk's Use

Taxed _____
Return recorded _____

_____
Notary Public, _____ County,
_____. (or other competent officer.)

How to fill out the information sheet

INFORMATION FOR SERVICE OF PROCESS

FROM: _____ _____

Address _____

Phone(s) _____

TO: _____

_____

_____

RE: In the Matter of the Marriage of:

_____, Petitioner,

and _____, Respondent.

Cause No _____

In the _____ District Court of

_____County, Texas

Dear Sir:

Enclosed are copies of a Petition and Citation, and a money order for
$_____.

The enclosed papers MUST be served within 90 days of the date of issuance
of the Citation in order to be valid. The Return portion of the Citation
must, of course, be completely and accurately filled out and signed.

NOTE TO OFFICERS OUTSIDE THE STATE OF TEXAS:
The signature of the officer delivering the Citation and Petition MUST be
sworn and Notarized in order to be effective in Texas.

INFORMATION FOR SERVICE OF PROCESS:

Person to Be Served:_____

Address- Residence:_____

_____

Work:_____

Other:_____

Physical Description:_____

_____

COMMENTS:

Your name, address and phone number

Name and address of sheriff or constable

Fill in as in the caption on your Petition

You will have called ahead to ask how much the cost will be

Give the fullest, most complete and current information available

7. The Decree

What it is

After listening to your testimony at the hearing, the judge will verbally make findings and issue orders — that's the judgment. The clerk will take notes of that judgment on the docket sheet as evidence of the decision. The Decree is a typed statement of the judgment, signed by the judge and entered into the record books by the clerk.

In all cases with children, there will be an order to the employer of the person paying child support to withhold income (see Chapters D and 8). This is the Order to Withhold Earnings. The Request to Issue Withholding Order is a simple request that the clerk serve the Withholding Order on a named employer.

Since you almost always get what you expect in uncontested cases, it is customary to prepare the Decree before the hearing and take it with you so it can be signed by the judge at that time. In the odd case where the judge decides differently from your Decree, you may have to prepare a different Decree that accurately reflects the judge's order and send it in (through the clerk) at a later time for signing. This is why you should make extra copies of the blank Decree before filling it out — you might need another blank later.

How to fill it out

Make extra copies of the blank Decree, then fill out the forms as shown in the illustrations on the next pages.

Then what?

If you are going to have an approved Decree (see Chapter E), have your spouse initial all crossed-out parts and sign the last page as shown in the illustration in Chapter E, section 1, *then* make copies with your spouse's signature on it. If you have a Marital Settlement Contract, attach a copy to each copy of the Decree. If you use the Withholding Order (see Chapter 8), attach a copy to each copy of the Decree. Be sure to keep all originals together. Do not attach the Request to Issue Withholding Order to the Decree — it goes separately to the clerk.

Check over the forms for accuracy and make four copies of each on a high-quality copy machine. Take all originals and copies of all forms with you to the hearing.

Notes for the first page

ID Numbers for your spouse: If you don't know your spouse's driver's license number or social security number, and if you can't get them, type in "unknown" in the blanks on the form.

How to fill out the Decree

First page

Cause No._____

IN THE MATTER OF THE MARRIAGE OF:

_____, Petitioner

AND

_____, Respondent

AND IN THE INTEREST OF

_____

_____CHILD(REN)

IN THE DISTRICT COURT

OF _____COUNTY

_____JUDICIAL DISTRICT

DECREE OF DIVORCE

On the _____ day of _____, 20___, final hearing was held in this cause.

Petitioner, _____, Soc.Sec.No. _____, Driver's License No. _____,appeared in person, pro se, and announced ready for trial.

Respondent, _____, Soc.Sec.No. _____, Driver's License No. _____.

...was duly and properly cited by personal service and failed to appear.

...waived issuance and service of citation by waiver duly filed and did not otherwise appear.

The making of a record of testimony was waived by the parties with consent of the Court.

Because a jury was not demanded by either party, the Court tried the cause.

The Court, having examined the pleadings and heard the evidence finds that all necessary residence requirements and prerequisites of law have been legally satisfied; that this Court has personal jurisdiction of the parties and of the subject matter of this cause; and that the material allegations of the petition are true.

DIVORCE DECREE

THE COURT FINDS that Petitioner and Respondent were married, and that their marriage had become insupportable because of discord or conflict of personalities which destroyed the legitimate ends of the marriage without any reasonable expectation of reconciliation.

THE COURT ORDERS AND DECREES that the marriage of Petitioner and Respondent is dissolved and that they are hereby divorced.

Page 1 of __

Callouts:

- Fill out caption as shown on page 73
- Date of hearing
- Your name, social security and driver's license number
- Your spouse's name, social security and driver's license number
- Cross out this part if a court reporter makes a record of your hearing
- Use this part if your spouse was served with papers
- Use this part if your spouse signed a waiver
- Put in total number of pages in Decree

Notes for the second page

Employee retirement benefits

Read Chapter B, section 3d: Pension and retirement plans.

- Use the first part if there is no community interest in any plan.

- Use the second part if you want to have the court put off decisions about the value and division of some plan until a later date. Remember that if you wait longer than two years, you may lose your rights!

If there is more than one plan, then type a new second page and use the relevant paragraphs as many times as necessary.

Separate property

- Use the first part if there was no separate property listed in the Petition.

- Use the second part if you itemized separate property in the Petition. List it here in a similar manner (see instructions on next page for listing property).

How to fill out the Decree

Second page

Cross out parts that do not apply to your case

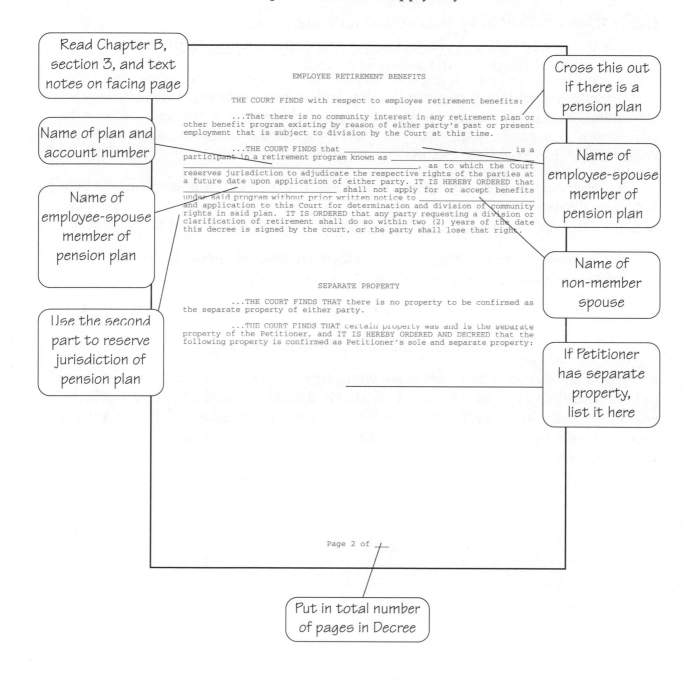

Read Chapter B, section 3, and text notes on facing page

Name of plan and account number

Name of employee-spouse member of pension plan

Use the second part to reserve jurisdiction of pension plan

Cross this out if there is a pension plan

Name of employee-spouse member of pension plan

Name of non-member spouse

If Petitioner has separate property, list it here

Put in total number of pages in Decree

EMPLOYEE RETIREMENT BENEFITS

THE COURT FINDS with respect to employee retirement benefits:

...That there is no community interest in any retirement plan or other benefit program existing by reason of either party's past or present employment that is subject to division by the Court at this time.

...THE COURT FINDS that _____ is a participant in a retirement program known as _____ _____, as to which the Court reserves jurisdiction to adjudicate the respective rights of the parties at a future date upon application of either party. IT IS HEREBY ORDERED that _____ shall not apply for or accept benefits under said program without prior written notice to _____ and application to this Court for determination and division of community rights in said plan. IT IS ORDERED that any party requesting a division or clarification of retirement shall do so within two (2) years of the date this decree is signed by the court, or the party shall lose that right.

SEPARATE PROPERTY

...THE COURT FINDS THAT there is no property to be confirmed as the separate property of either party.

...THE COURT FINDS THAT certain property was and is the separate property of the Petitioner, and IT IS HEREBY ORDERED AND DECREED that the following property is confirmed as Petitioner's sole and separate property:

Page 2 of ___

Notes for the third page

How to list the property

Use the first option if you have no property or debts to divide. Draw lines through the second and third options.

Use the second option if you and your spouse have a marital settlement contract, then draw lines through the first and third options.

If you listed property on your Petition and it was not later divided by written agreement, then it will be divided by the judge, probably just as you request. Use the third option, list property the way you want it awarded (usually as requested in the Petition) and don't forget to include income taxes and all debts.

Number each item in this listing (not necessarily the same number as in the Petition). Use the same description as in the Petition, but you need not put down the value of items. Give the license and vehicle ID number for any vehicles that are awarded.

Real Estate: If real property is awarded, you should use language like this when you list it:

(item number) "The following real property, including any escrow funds, prepaid insurance, utility deposits, keys, and title documents: (give common and full legal description just as in the Petition)."

If you use our form and there is not enough room for all of the property and debts to be listed, then type in: "As listed on attached sheet entitled 'Property Division,' which is wholly incorporated here for all purposes by reference." Then, on a blank sheet, type the heading "Property Division," type your list on it and staple a copy to each copy of the Decree.

How to fill out the Decree

Third page

Cross out parts that do not apply to your case

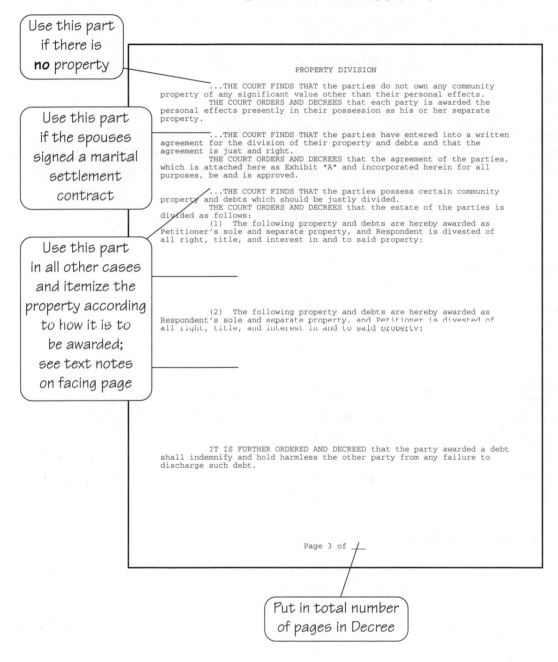

Use this part if there is **no** property

Use this part if the spouses signed a marital settlement contract

Use this part in all other cases and itemize the property according to how it is to be awarded; see text notes on facing page

PROPERTY DIVISION

...THE COURT FINDS THAT the parties do not own any community property of any significant value other than their personal effects.
THE COURT ORDERS AND DECREES that each party is awarded the personal effects presently in their possession as his or her separate property.

...THE COURT FINDS THAT the parties have entered into a written agreement for the division of their property and debts and that the agreement is just and right.
THE COURT ORDERS AND DECREES that the agreement of the parties, which is attached here as Exhibit "A" and incorporated herein for all purposes, be and is approved.

...THE COURT FINDS THAT the parties possess certain community property and debts which should be justly divided.
THE COURT ORDERS AND DECREES that the estate of the parties is divided as follows:
(1) The following property and debts are hereby awarded as Petitioner's sole and separate property, and Respondent is divested of all right, title, and interest in and to said property:

(2) The following property and debts are hereby awarded as Respondent's sole and separate property, and Petitioner is divested of all right, title, and interest in and to said property:

IT IS FURTHER ORDERED AND DECREED that the party awarded a debt shall indemnify and hold harmless the other party from any failure to discharge such debt.

Page 3 of

Put in total number of pages in Decree

Notes for the fourth page

If you are *not* going to ask for court-ordered spousal maintenance and you *do* have children, discard this page and don't use it at all.

If you are *not* going to ask for court-ordered spousal maintenance and you *do not* have children, you might find it easier to retype the bottom paragraph about children at the bottom of page three of the Decree. Otherwise you have to draw lines through the entire maintenance sections on this page. Discard pages five through ten of the Decree and go straight to page eleven.

If you *are* going to ask the court to award spousal maintenance, choose the statements that apply to your case and cross out ones that do not. (You cannot apply for maintenance if your divorce was filed before September 1, 1995.) See Chapter D for more information about the alimony law. If your spouse is already willing to pay support, you would be better off making support part of a written marital settlement contract because in a written contract, you can make it for any amount and length of time you want. Court-ordered maintenance has many limitations.

Notes for the fifth page

If a child has no social security number, you will have to contact the Social Security Office to get one, as it is necessary for the enforcement of your support orders. Put in drivers license numbers for any children who have them. For children that don't, type in "none."

As you read in Chapter C, Texas law now presumes that joint custody (Joint Managing Conservatorship) is best for children of divorce. In actual fact, it is mostly terminology and not that different from the old Managing/Possessory Conservatorship. We have left both options in the Decree, but are not sure how the courts will respond at this point. If you have good reasons not to have Joint Managing Conservatorship, be prepared to tell them to the judge.

Notes for the sixth page

This is where you get to tailor your conservatorship plan. Use the names of the spouses in the blanks provided (rather than Petitioner and Respondent) to establish which parent has the named rights and responsibilities. In Joint Managing Conservatorships, many of these blanks will be filled in with both parents' names. The parent who has the right to establish the primary residence of the children will be the Managing Conservator, or in Joint Conservatorships the one the children are with most of the time and who receives child support.

How to fill out the Decree

Fourth page

Cross out parts that do not apply to your case

Use at least one of these; you **can** use both if they are both true

You must use at least one of these; cross out any that are not true

Put Petitioner or Respondent in appropriate blanks

Amount of spousal support to be paid

You can only use this one if you are disabled or have a disabled child to care for

Date payments are to begin

Put Petitioner or Respondent in appropriate blanks

Put in total number of pages in Decree

MAINTENANCE

The Court finds maintenance should be awarded on the following grounds:

_____ ...Petitioner and Respondent were married at least ten (10) years.

_____ ...Respondent was convicted of or received deferred adjudication for a family violence crime within two years from the date of the filing of this Petition.

and Petitioner lacks sufficient property, including property distributed after this divorce, to provide for Petitioner's minimum reasonable needs; and Petitioner

_____ ...clearly lacks the earning ability in the labor market adequate to provide for Petitioner's minimum reasonable needs.

_____ ...is unable to support him/herself through employment because of an incapcitating physical or mental disability.

_____ ...is the custodian of a child who requires substantial care and personal supervision because of a physcal or mental disability which makes it necessary that Petitioner not be employed outside of the home.

THEREFORE, IT IS ORDERED _____ (paying party) pay to _____ (receiving party) for spousal maintenance the sum of $_____ per month, due and payable beginning_____, 20____ and continuing on the same day of each month thereafter until

either party dies; or
the receiving party remarries. This order for maintenance shall continue for

_____ ... for ____ months not to exceed thirty six (36) months.

_____ ... for an indefinite period.

IT IS FURTHER ORDERED that all payments shall be made by _____ (paying party) to _____ (receiving party) at any address designated in writing by _____ (receiving party).

CHILDREN

_____ ...THE COURT FINDS that there is no unmarried child of the marriage under eighteen years of age and none is expected.

Page 4 of ___

7. The Decree

How to fill out the Decree

Fifth page

Cross out parts that do not apply to your case

THE COURT FINDS that the following unmarried children under the age of eighteen were born to or adopted by the parties to the marriage and that no other is expected:

Name: _____ Sex: ___ Age: ____ Birthdate: _____
Present residence: _____
Birthplace: _____ SSN _____ DL # _____

Name: _____ Sex: ___ Age: ____ Birthdate: _____
Present residence: _____
Birthplace: _____ SSN _____ DL # _____

Name: _____ Sex: ___ Age: ____ Birthdate: _____
Present residence: _____
Birthplace: _____ SSN _____ DL # _____

Name: _____ Sex: ___ Age: ____ Birthdate: _____
Present residence: _____
Birthplace: _____ SSN _____ DL # _____

Name: _____ Sex: ___ Age: ____ Birthdate: _____
Present residence: _____
Birthplace: _____ SSN _____ DL # _____

THE COURT FINDS that the children do not own or possess any property other than their personal effects.

CONSERVATORSHIP

...THE COURT FINDS that the parties have made a written agreement concerning conservatorship of the child(ren) and that it is in the child(ren)'s best interest.

THE COURT FINDS, after considering the circumstances, that the following orders are in the best interest of the child(ren):

THE COURT ORDERS AND DECREES that

... _____ and _____ are appointed Joint Managing Conservators of the child(ren)

... _____ is appointed the Sole Managing Conservator of the child(ren) and _____ is appointed Possessory Conservator of the child(ren)

with all the rights and duties of a parent <u>at all times</u>, including: the right to receive information from the other parent concerning the health, education and welfare of the child(ren); to confer with the other parent to the extent possible before making decisions concerning the health, educa-tion and welfare of the child(ren); of access to medical, dental, psycho-logical and educational records of the child(ren); to consult with a physician, dentist or psychologist of the child(ren); to consult with school officials concerning the

Page 5 of ___

Callout (top right): Give information requested for each child, including complete address; see notes

Callout: If you will have **joint** custody, put the parents' names here

Callout: If you will **not** have joint custody, put the Managing Conservator's name here,

Callout: and the Possessory Conservator's name here

Callout: Put in total number of pages in Decree

Privacy: In cases where you need to protect the location of a party or a child, you can omit any of the following from all pa-pers filed in your divorce: the child's sex, place of birth, place of residence; and the parents' ages and places of residence.

How to fill out the Decree

Sixth page

Cross out parts that do not apply to your case

Put both parents' names in these blanks

Only one parent can establish primary residence of the children; see notes

Fill in the parent's (or parents') names who will have each of these rights

child(ren); to consult with school officials concerning the child(ren)'s welfare and educational status, including school activities; to be designated on the child's records as a person to be notified in case of an emergency; to consent to medical, dental and surgical treatment during an emergency involving an immediate danger to the health and safety of the child; to inherit from and through the child(ren); and to manage the estate of the child(ren) to the extent the estate was created by the parent or the parent's family.

THE COURT ORDERS AND DECREES that _____ and _____, shall each have the following rights and duties during the period each has possession of the child(ren): the duty of care, control, protection and reasonable discipline of the child(ren); the duty to support the child(ren), including providing clothing, food, shelter and medical and dental care not involving an invasive procedure; the right to consent for the child(ren) to medical and dental care not involving an invasive procedure; the right to consent for the child(ren) to medical, dental and surgical treatment during an emergency involving immediate danger to the health and safety of the child(ren); and the right to direct the moral and religious training of the child(ren).

THE COURT ORDERS AND DECREES that each parent has a duty to inform the other parent in a timely manner of significant information concerning the health, education and welfare of the child(ren).

....THE COURT ORDERS AND DECREES that _____ shall have the right to establish the primary residence (domicile) of the children.
....THE COURT ORDERS AND DECREES that the residence of the child(ren) shall remain in _____ County and any contiguous county thereto until further order of the Court.
....THE COURT ORDERS AND DECREES the child(ren)'s primary residence may be established by _____ without restriction.

THE COURT FURTHER ORDERS AND DECREES that each party as named below shall have the following rights and duties exclusively:

_____ shall have the right to consent to medical, dental and surgical treatment involving invasive procedures, and to consent to psychiatric and psychological treatment;
_____ shall have the right to receive and give receipt for periodic payments for the support of the child(ren) (child support) and to hold or disburse these funds for the benefit of the child(ren);
_____ shall have the right to represent the child(ren) in legal action and to make other decisions of substantial legal significance concerning the child(ren);
_____ shall have the right to make decisions concerning the child(ren)'s education;
_____ shall have the right to the services and earnings of the child(ren); and

except when a guardian of the child(ren)'s estate or guardian or attorney at litem has been appointed for the child(ren),
shall have the right to act as an agent of the child(ren) in relation to the child(ren)'s estate if the child(ren)'s action is required by a state, the United States or a foreign government.

Page 6 of ____

Put in total number of pages in Decree

Notes for the seventh page

First, carefully read Chapter C, section 3 and the Standard Schedule for Possession of Minor Children in the forms section.

- Use the first part if you type your own Decree from scratch, then insert your schedule for possession at this point. Use wording either from the standard schedule in the forms section, or terms set forth in a written agreement between the parties.

- Use the second part if you use our forms and plan to attach a schedule at the end of the Decree. Attach either the Possession Schedule from this book, or your own terms copied from an agreement between the spouses, which you would also attach.

- Use the third part only if there is a child under the age of three, *and* if, because of the child's age, you want some alternate terms until the child's third birthday. Put your alternate terms either directly in the Decree (first option under this part) or, (second option under this part) on a separate schedule headed "Schedule for Possession of Children Under Three Years." Use the standard schedule in the forms section as a guide for wording of your terms.

How to fill out the Decree

Seventh page

Cross out parts that do not apply to your case

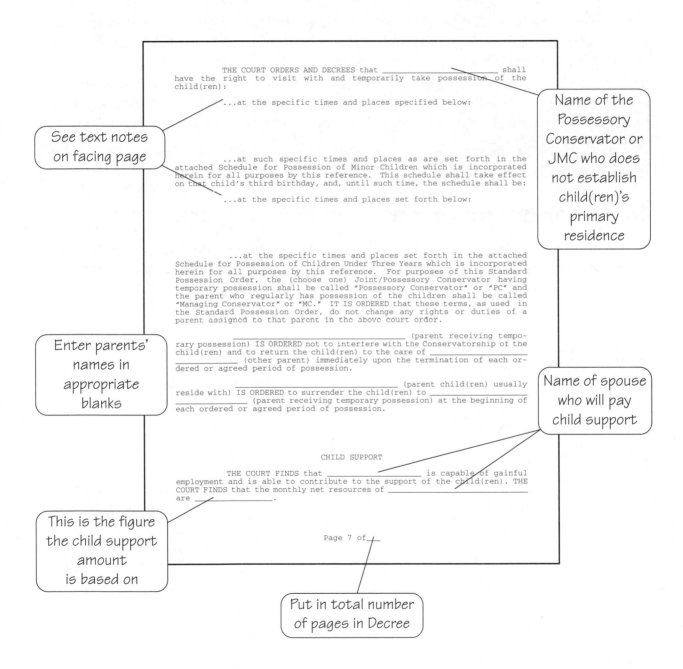

THE COURT ORDERS AND DECREES that _____ shall have the right to visit with and temporarily take possession of the child(ren):

...at the specific times and places specified below:

See text notes on facing page

Name of the Possessory Conservator or JMC who does not establish child(ren)'s primary residence

...at such specific times and places as are set forth in the attached Schedule for Possession of Minor Children which is incorporated herein for all purposes by this reference. This schedule shall take effect on that child's third birthday, and, until such time, the schedule shall be:

...at the specific times and places set forth below:

...at the specific times and places set forth in the attached Schedule for Possession of Children Under Three Years which is incorporated herein for all purposes by this reference. For purposes of this Standard Possession Order, the (choose one) Joint/Possessory Conservator having temporary possession shall be called "Possessory Conservator" or "PC" and the parent who regularly has possession of the children shall be called "Managing Conservator" or "MC." IT IS ORDERED that these terms, as used in the Standard Possession Order, do not change any rights or duties of a parent assigned to that parent in the above court order.

Enter parents' names in appropriate blanks

_____ (parent receiving temporary possession) IS ORDERED not to interfere with the Conservatorship of the child(ren) and to return the child(ren) to the care of _____ (other parent) immediately upon the termination of each ordered or agreed period of possession.

_____ (parent child(ren) usually reside with) IS ORDERED to surrender the child(ren) to _____ (parent receiving temporary possession) at the beginning of each ordered or agreed period of possession.

Name of spouse who will pay child support

CHILD SUPPORT

THE COURT FINDS that _____ is capable of gainful employment and is able to contribute to the support of the child(ren). THE COURT FINDS that the monthly net resources of _____ are _____.

This is the figure the child support amount is based on

Page 7 of __

Put in total number of pages in Decree

Notes for the eighth page

Don't forget, if the Obligee is ordered to pay for health insurance, an additional amount can be added to child support to cover the cost of the insurance. See the discussion in Chapter D.

If there is only one child, draw lines through the paragraph after Item 6 that begins "Thereafter . . ." If there are two children, keep the "Thereafter" paragraph in, and use the child support chart in Chapter D to find the amount child support will be after the first child becomes emancipated. If there are more than two children, repeat the same paragraph for each one, reducing child support by the percentage shown in the chart until there is only one child left.

In the bottom paragraph you show what percentage each parent will pay for unreimbursed health care. Be sure the two figures total 100%.

Notes for the ninth page (not pictured here)

This page is just a long list of admonishments and warnings about each parent keeping each other, the Court and the State Case Registry Office informed of any changes in address, phone or employment as long as there is a child support obligation.

How to fill out the Decree

Eighth page

Cross out parts that do not apply to your case

> Name of spouse who will pay support

> Name of spouse who will receive support

> Total amount to be paid each month

> Use this part if there is more than one child being supported; see notes on facing page

> Use this part if you have a handicapped child

> Put in the date payments are to begin

> See text notes on facing page for filling out this section

> Put in total number of pages in Decree

THE COURT ORDERS AND DECREES that _____, hereafter Obligor, is obligated to pay and, subject to the income withholding provisions specified below, shall pay to _____ hereafter Obligee, child support in the total amount of $_____ per month, payable beginning on the _____ day of _____, 20___, and a like payment being due and payable on the same day of each subsequent month, continuing thereafter until the earliest of any of the following conditions occur for any child:

1) the child reaches the age of 18 years, and thereafter, so long as the child is fully enrolled in an accredited primary or secondary school in a program leading toward a high school diploma, until the end of the school term in which the child graduates;
2) the child marries;
3) the child dies;
4) the child's disabilities are otherwise removed for general purposes;
5) the child is otherwise emancipated; or
6) until further order of the court.

Thereafter, Obligor is ORDERED AND DECREED to pay to Obligee child support of $_____ per month, with the first payment being due and payable on the _____ day of each month until the first month following the date of the next occurrence of one of the events specified above.

...THE COURT FINDS THAT _____ is a child in need of support as defined in section 154.302 of the Texas Family Code, and therefore THE COURT ORDERS AND DECREES that of the above amount ordered for child support, and notwithstanding any other language above, the amount of $_____ per month for the support of said child shall be a continuing obligation until further order of the Court.

IT IS FURTHER ORDERED that for the term of the child support obligation for each child,

...as additional child support, Obligor shall carry and maintain medical health insurance for the benefit of said child.

...Obligee shall carry and maintain medical health coverage for the benefit of said child.

...Obligor will reimburse Obligee for amounts Obligee pays for medical health coverage for said child, and that amount has been included in the child support figure above.

IT IS FURTHER ORDERED that Obligor shall pay ___ percent and Obligee shall pay ___ percent of the child(ren)'s medical expenses that are not reimbursed by insurance.

Page 8 of ____

Notes for the tenth page

The 1997 Legislature decided that income withholding must be ordered in *every* case that orders child support. It does not matter if the obligor is unemployed, self-employed, or even long gone, you still must get withholding ordered in your Decree. The order remains on file and can be "issued" later on if the obligor gets a job that support can be withheld from. The order is valid until all support (and any interest for arrearages) is paid in full.

Note: Before filling out this part, call the clerk to ask the name and address for the office or registry used by your court for the collection of support payments. Call that office and ask for an account number to be used on your withholding form.

Notes for the eleventh page *(not pictured here)*

Although some of this information appears in other places, this page must be included *if you have children* to comply with the Family Code. If you have more than two children, photocopy this page before you start filling it out so you will have blank spaces for the additional children. Put your information in the first set of blanks, your spouse's in the second set, and information about the children in as many of the next sets as required. *If you do* not *have children, you don't use this page at all.*

If there is a history of family violence, you can request the Court allow you to omit this information from the Decree. You will need to testify to the judge about the reason the addresses for you and your children should remain secret from your spouse. You will also have to notify your spouse of the hearing (see Chapter 10B, Getting into Court, page 130). If you want to request this omission, add this language at the bottom of the tenth page of the Decree:

> *The Court finds, after hearing evidence, that the requirement of disclosing the address, telephone number, place of employment and telephone number of a party or of the child(ren) will cause the party or the child(ren) harassment, abuse, serious harm or injury. Therefore, IT IS ORDERED the disclosure requirement is WAIVED and _____ is excused from compliance with section 105.006 of the Texas Family Code.*

How to fill out the Decree

Tenth page

INCOME WITHHOLDING AND PAYMENT OF SUPPORT

THE COURT ORDERS AND DECREES that the above child support obligation shall be discharged, pro tanto, by income withholding. The attached "Employer's Order To Withhold Earnings," which was signed by the Court on this date, is wholly incorporated herein for all purposes by reference, and any employer of Obligor IS ORDERED to withhold income according to the terms set forth therein or until further order of the Court.

IT IS FURTHER ORDERED that Obligor is ordered to claim no fewer than the actual number of his/her dependents on the W-4 form.

IT IS FURTHER ORDERED that all amounts withheld and paid in accordance with said order shall constitute a credit against the child support obligation. If the amount so withheld and paid is less than 100% of the amount ordered to be paid by this decree, the balance due remains an obligation of Obligor, and it IS ORDERED that Obligor pay the balance due directly to the registry, office, or person specified below.

IT IS ORDERED that all payments for child support be made through:

_____

and then promptly remitted to the party receiving child support for the support of the children.

> Give the name and address of office through which payments are to be made

IT IS ORDERED that, upon request of a prosecuting attorney, the Attorney General, the Obligee or the Obligor, the clerk of this Court shall cause a certified copy of the "Employer's Order To Withhold Earnings" to be delivered to any employer. IT IS FURTHER ORDERED that the clerk of this Court shall attach a copy of Chapter 158, Subchapter C of the Texas Family Code for the information of any employer.

Page 10 of ____

> Put in total number of pages in Decree

How to fill out the Decree

Twelfth page

Cross out parts that do not apply to your case

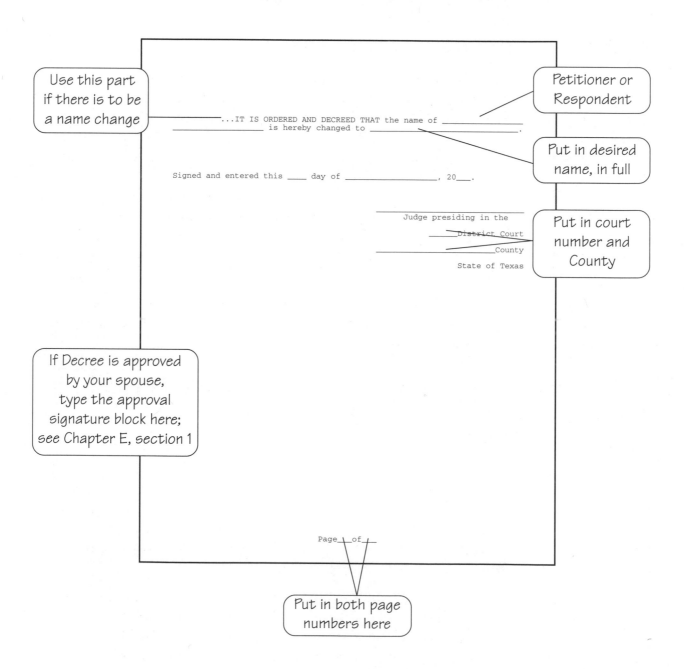

Use this part if there is to be a name change

Petitioner or Respondent

...IT IS ORDERED AND DECREED THAT the name of _____ _____ is hereby changed to _____.

Put in desired name, in full

Signed and entered this ____ day of _____, 20___.

_____
Judge presiding in the
_____District Court
_____County
State of Texas

Put in court number and County

If Decree is approved by your spouse, type the approval signature block here; see Chapter E, section 1

Page___of___

Put in both page numbers here

8. The Withholding forms

What they are

Use these forms if child support or spousal maintenance will be ordered.

A. Which withholding order to use

1. Child Support with or without spousal maintenance. If child support will be ordered, you *must* fill out the **Order/Notice to Withhold Income for Child Support** and take it to the hearing with your Decree. If spousal maintenance was also ordered, included it here, but only if the recipient is the managing conservator of the child for whom support is owed and the child resides with him/her. Note: income withholding for spousal maintenance can be ordered if payments are imposed by a court, but *not* for spousal maintenance agreed by the parties unless the contract specifically permits it. Even if the Obligee is self-employed, unemployed or unfindable, you must nonetheless get withholding ordered. The order will remain on file until the obligor has wages that support can be withheld from or until the entire support obligation, including arrearages, is completely paid.

2. Spousal Maintenance with no order for child support. If you will have an order for spousal maintenance and no order for child support, you *must* fill out and file the **Employer's Order to Withhold Earnings for Spousal Maintenance**.

B. The Request to Issue Order to Withhold Earnings for Support

When you are ready to have the Clerk's Office send your withholding order to the Obligor's employer, use this **Request to Issue** form. File it with the District Clerk and pay a nominal filing fee, about $20. If the Obligor changes jobs, you can file a new **Request to Issue** form naming the new employer. You might make an agreement with your spouse that this form will not be filed as long as support payments are not a week late or thirty days late, or some such time period. In cases where the supported children are receiving public assistance, this form *must* be issued.

The **Employer's Order to Withhold Earnings for Spousal Maintenance** and **Request for Issuance of Employer's Order — Spousal Maintenance** must be filled out if you have spousal maintenance in your decree. The judge will sign the **Employer's Order** at the hearing and then you file the **Request to Issue** with the District Clerk and pay a nominal filing fee (around $20). If the Payor changes jobs and does not notify his employer, you can file a new Request for Issuance to his/her new employer.

How to fill out the Order/Notice to Withhold Income for Child Support

For the caption information, on the second line, fill in the county where your case is filed. The third line (date of Order/Notice) is the date the judge signed the Order/Notice. On the fourth line, court/case number, enter the number of your court and then the number of your case.

For the section beginning "$_____ per _____ in current support", enter

a) the total amount of child support, then

b) past due support (not applicable in a new divorce), then

c) the dollar amount for medical support if Obligor is not providing health insurance and the Obligee is, then

d) spousal maintenance (if requested), then

e) add up these amounts and enter the total of all support in the line that says "for a total of $____ per ____ to be forwarded to payee below."

It will be better if you express these amounts as a monthly figure; it will make things easier for you and the employer in the long run. If payor is on some other time period, here's how to do the conversion. If the amount of support you are dealing with is a weekly amount, multiply it by 4.33 to get the monthly amount. If your support is a biweekly amount (every two weeks), multiply it by 2.17 to get the monthly amount. If the amount of support is a semimonthly amount (twice a month), multiply it by 2 to get the monthly amount.

Now, for the section beginning "You do not have to vary your pay cycle . . ." take the grand total of all support due and multiply it to break it down for the employer's pay period. For the "per monthly pay period", write in the amount due monthly. For the "per semimonthly pay period (twice per month)", multiply the monthly amount by .50. For the "per biweekly pay period (every two weeks)", multiply the monthly amount by .4615. Finally, for the "per weekly pay period", multiply the monthly amount by .2308.

For the sentence beginning "Make it payable to:", enter your name and the case number.

For the sentence beginning "Send Check to:", put in the address for payments provided to you by your local child support registry. The District Clerk's office can tell you how to contact the child support registry. It may be a local address or the Office of the Attorney General Central Disbursement Unit.

Order/Notice to Withhold Income for Child Support

Page 1

Note: "Employer" in the instructions also refers to any other withholder upon whom the order might be served.

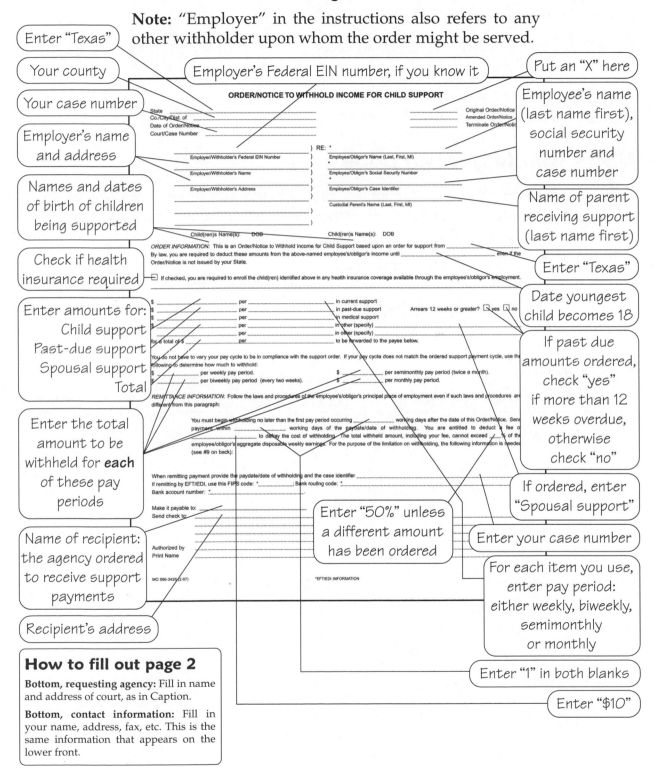

Enter "Texas"

Your county

Your case number

Employer's name and address

Names and dates of birth of children being supported

Check if health insurance required

Enter amounts for:
Child support
Past-due support
Spousal support
Total

Enter the total amount to be withheld for **each** of these pay periods

Name of recipient: the agency ordered to receive support payments

Recipient's address

Employer's Federal EIN number, if you know it

Put an "X" here

Employee's name (last name first), social security number and case number

Name of parent receiving support (last name first)

Enter "Texas"

Date youngest child becomes 18

If past due amounts ordered, check "yes" if more than 12 weeks overdue, otherwise check "no"

If ordered, enter "Spousal support"

Enter your case number

For each item you use, enter pay period: either weekly, biweekly, semimonthly or monthly

Enter "1" in both blanks

Enter "$10"

Enter "50%" unless a different amount has been ordered

How to fill out page 2

Bottom, requesting agency: Fill in name and address of court, as in Caption.

Bottom, contact information: Fill in your name, address, fax, etc. This is the same information that appears on the lower front.

How to fill out the Employer's Order to Withhold Earnings for Spousal Maintenance

Note 1. Fill out the Caption just like all the other forms.

Note 2. Fill in the requested information for the Payor (the person ordered to pay spousal maintenance) and the Payee (the person receiving spousal maintenance).

Note 3: Privacy. In cases where you need to protect the location of a party, you can omit the party's place of place of residence.

Notes for the second page

Under "Order to Withhold", fill in all four blanks in this section. At line (1), enter the full monthly amount of spousal maintenance. For line (2), multiply the full monthly amount by .50 and enter the result here. For line (3) multiply by .4615 and for line (4) multiply by .2308.

In the next blank, enter the date the court ordered the spousal maintenance to terminate. If the court ordered maintenance for 24 months, enter the last day of the 24th month from the date the court signs this order.

Then what?

Make four copies and take them to court with your Decree. Be sure to keep the originals together. You will take these with you to the hearing.

Employer's Order to Withhold Earnings for Spousal Maintenance

First page

Fill out caption as shown on page 73

Cause No. _____

IN THE MATTER OF THE MARRIAGE OF:

_____, Petitioner

AND

_____, Respondent

IN THE DISTRICT COURT

OF _____ COUNTY

_____ JUDICIAL DISTRICT

**EMPLOYER'S ORDER TO WITHHOLD
EARNINGS FOR SPOUSAL MAINTENANCE**

The Court ORDERS you, the employer of PAYOR to withhold income from his/her disposable earnings from this employment as follows:

PAYOR
Name: _____

Address: _____

Social Security number: _____

Information about the person who will be paying support, here called the "Payor"

PAYEE
Name: _____

Address: _____

Social Security number: _____

Information about the person who will be receiving support, here called the "Payee"

Withholding from Earnings for Spousal Maintenance

The Court ORDERS that any employer of PAYOR shall begin withholding from his/her disposable earnings no later than the first pay period following the date this order is served on that employer.

Method of Payment

The Court ORDERS the employer to pay all amounts withheld on each payday to PAYEE at the address stated above, or at any address provided to you by PAYEE in writing.

Note: You can omit your address if you fear to have Payor know it.

Employer's Order to Withhold Earnings
for Spousal Maintenance

Second page

Order to Withhold

The Court ORDERS the employer to withhold the following amounts from the earnings of PAYOR:

(1) $_____ on current spousal maintenance if PAYOR is paid monthly

(2) $_____ on current spousal maintenance, if PAYOR is paid twice monthly

(3) $_____ on current spousal maintenance, if PAYOR is paid every other week

(4) $_____ on current spousal maintenance, if PAYOR is paid every week

    The Court ORDERS the employer to withhold the above amount until _____.

Calculating Disposable Earnings

    The employer shall calculate PAYOR's disposable earnings, which are subject to withholding for child support, as follows:

    1. Determine the "earnings" of PAYOR, which means compensation paid or payable for personal services, whether called wages, salary, compensation received as an independent contractor, overtime pay, severance pay, commission, bonus, or otherwise, including periodic payments pursuant to a pension, an annuity, workers' compensation, a disability and retirement program, and unemployment benefits;

    2. Subtract the following sums to calculate PAYOR's "disposable earnings":

        a. any amounts required by law to be withheld, that is, federal income tax and federal FICA or OASI tax (Social Security) and Railroad Retirement Act contributions;
        b. union dues;
        c. nondiscretionary retirement contributions by PAYOR; and
        d. medical, hospitalization, and disability insurance coverage for PAYOR and payor's children.

Notice of Change of Employment

    The Court ORDERS the employer to notify the Court and PAYEE within seven days of the date that PAYOR terminates employment. The Court ORDERS the employer to provide PAYOR's last known address and the name and address of his new employer, if known.

    SIGNED on _____.

_____
JUDGE PRESIDING

> You must put a number on all four lines. See text note for how to calculate.

> Enter date or time period when support ends. See text note.

How to fill out the Request to Issue Withholding Order(s)

First of all, make a copy of the blank form to keep in your file. If the Obligor/Payor changes jobs in the future, you will need to fill out another one to have sent to the new employer.

Fill in the caption just like you did for all the other forms.

Fill in the blanks as illustrated on the next page.

Then what?

Make four copies of the form. You do not have to present these at the hearing, but keep them in your file anyway.

If you are going to order withholding for either child support or spousal maintenance at your first opportunity, then take this form to the clerk of the court right after the Decree and Withholding Order(s) are signed so the Withholding order(s) can be served on the employer. You may have to pay a fee of $20 or so per order at this time.

If for some reason you are not going to ask the clerk to serve the order(s) on the employer right now, just keep this form in your file until the time comes that you do want the Withholding Order issued.

In all cases where children are receiving public assistance, the Withholding Order for child support *must* be issued by the clerk as soon as support is ordered in your Decree.

Request to Issue Withholding Order(s)

Fill out caption as shown on page 73

Cause No. _____

IN THE MATTER OF THE MARRIAGE OF:

_____, Petitioner

AND

_____, Respondent

AND IN THE INTEREST OF

_____

_____,

CHILD(REN)

IN THE DISTRICT COURT

OF _____ COUNTY

_____ JUDICIAL DISTRICT

REQUEST TO ISSUE
EMPLOYER'S ORDER TO WITHHOLD
EARNINGS FOR CHILD SUPPORT OR SPOUSAL MAINTENANCE

To the Clerk of the Court:

Please issue a certified copy of the following order(s) in this cause:
(check which order(s) should be issued)

_____ Order/Notice to Withhold from Earnings for Child Support, signed
by the Court on _____ [date court signed order]

_____ Employer's Order to Withholding Earnings for Spousal Maintenance,
signed by the Court on _____ [date court signed order].

And deliver the order to:

Obligor/Payor's Employer: _____

Address: _____

City, State, ZIP _____

Submitted on _____.

_____
OBLIGEE/PAYEE

_____
OBLIGEE/PAYEE'S ADDRESS

Check one to show which witholding order you are requesting

Enter name and address of Payor's employer.

Do not enter your address if you fear to have the Payor know this. See note 3, page 120.

9. The Statistics Form

Information on Suit
Affecting the Family Relationship

What is it?

Although the court already has a file full of information about your divorce, they need this additional form to track and report the basics of your case to the Bureau of Vital Statistics. When there are children, the State Case Registry uses it for tracking support orders and payments. The Bureau of Vital Statistics uses the basic information about your divorce for their periodic statistical reports.

How to fill it out

Fill it out as shown on the next three pages.

Then what?

Make one copy of the completed form for your own files and take the original with you to the hearing. The clerk will ask for it at the right time.

Notes for the front side

There is no need to cross out unused sections on this form.

Section 1: The information for Item 1 comes from the caption on your divorce forms. At Item 2, check one of the top boxes to indicate whether or not your divorce involves children. At item 4, because you are representing yourself, enter your own name, phone and address. Your name should be followed by a comma and the words Pro Se. Leave box 4b blank

Section 2: Fill in all requested information. If no children, enter "0" at item 17.

Section 3: Fill in as many segments as you have children. If more than four children, attach an additional form marked "continuation" at the top and attach it to the original form. As children of divorce do not typically get new names, nor are they typically known by a prior name (a.k.a.), most people will leave items f and g blank.

Notes for the back side

Section 4: Must be completed if there is child support. "Obligee" is the parent receiving support and "Obligor #1" is the parent who pays support. Check box 25c or 25d to show if obligee is the husband or wife, then complete only items 31 and 32. Next, check box 33b or 33c to show if Obligor #1 is the husband or wife, then complete only items 39 to 43.

Section 5: Leave blank.

Section 6: Leave blank.

Information on Suit
Affecting the Family Relationship

Front side

See text notes for section 1

Check box to indicate whether or not there are children.

Fill in requested information. See text notes for Section 2.

Fill in the information for as many children as you have. See text notes for Section 3.

INFORMATION ON SUIT AFFECTING THE FAMILY RELATIONSHIP
(EXCLUDING ADOPTIONS)

SECTION I   GENERAL INFORMATION (REQUIRED)   STATE FILE NUMBER

1a. COUNTY_____ 1b. COURT NO. _____

1d. CAUSE NO. _____ 1e. DATE OF ORDER (mm/dd/yyyy) _____

2. HAS THERE BEEN A FINDING BY THE COURT OF: ☐ DOMESTIC VIOLENCE ? ☐ CHILD ABUSE ?

3. TYPE OF ORDER (CHECK ALL THAT APPLY):
☐ DIVORCE/ ANNULMENT <u>WITH</u> CHILDREN(Sec 1, 2, 3, 4)   ☐ DIVORCE/ ANNULMENT <u>WITHOUT</u> CHILDREN(Sec 1, 2)
☐ PATERNITY <u>WITH</u> CHILD SUPPORT (Sec 1, 3, 4, 5)   ☐ PATERNITY <u>WITHOUT</u> CHILD SUPPORT (Sec 1, 3, 5)
☐ CHILD SUPPORT OBLIGATION/MODIFICATION (Sec 1, 3, 4)   ☐ TERMINATION OF RIGHTS (Sec 1, 3, 6)
☐ CONSERVATORSHIP (Sec 1, 3)   ☐ OTHER (Specify)_____
☐ TRANSFER TO (Sec 1, 3) COUNTY_____ COURT NO. _____ STATE COURT ID# _____

4a. NAME OF ATTORNEY FOR PETITIONER   4b. ATTORNEY GENERAL ACCT/CASE #

4c. CURRENT MAILING ADDRESS: STREET & NO.   CITY   STATE   ZIP   4d. TELEPHONE NUMBER
(   )

SECTION 2 (IF APPLICABLE)   REPORT OF DIVORCE OR ANNULMENT OF MARRIAGE

HUSBAND
5. FIRST NAME   MIDDLE   LAST   SUFFIX   6. DATE OF BIRTH (mm/dd/yyyy)
7. PLACE OF BIRTH   CITY   STATE OR FOREIGN COUNTRY   8. RACE   9. SOCIAL SECURITY NUMBER
10. USUAL RESIDENCE   STREET NAME & NUMBER   CITY   STATE   ZIP

WIFE
11. FIRST NAME   MIDDLE   LAST   MAIDEN   12. DATE OF BIRTH (mm/dd/yyyy)
13. PLACE OF BIRTH   CITY   STATE OR FOREIGN COUNTRY   14. RACE   15. SOCIAL SECURITY NUMBER
16. USUAL RESIDENCE   STREET NAME & NUMBER   CITY   STATE   ZIP

17. NUMBER OF MINOR CHILDREN   18. DATE OF MARRIAGE (mm/dd/yyyy)   19. PLACE OF MARRIAGE   CITY   STATE   20 PETITIONER IS ☐ HUSBAND ☐ WIFE

SECTION 3 (IF APPLICABLE)   CHILDREN AFFECTED BY THIS SUIT

CHILD 1
21a. FIRST NAME   MIDDLE   LAST   SUFFIX   21b. DATE OF BIRTH (mm/dd/yyyy)
21c. SOCIAL SECURITY NUMBER   21d. SEX   21e. BIRTHPLACE CITY   COUNTY   STATE
21f. PRIOR NAME OF CHILD FIRST   MIDDLE   LAST   SUFFIX   21g. NEW NAME OF CHILD FIRST   MIDDLE   LAST   SUFFIX

CHILD 2
22a. FIRST NAME   MIDDLE   LAST   SUFFIX   22b. DATE OF BIRTH (mm/dd/yyyy)
22c. SOCIAL SECURITY NUMBER   22d. SEX   22e. BIRTHPLACE CITY   COUNTY   STATE
22f. PRIOR NAME OF CHILD FIRST   MIDDLE   LAST   SUFFIX   22g. NEW NAME OF CHILD FIRST   MIDDLE   LAST   SUFFIX

CHILD 3
23a. FIRST NAME   MIDDLE   LAST   SUFFIX   23b. DATE OF BIRTH (mm/dd/yyyy)
23c. SOCIAL SECURITY NUMBER   23d. SEX   23e. BIRTHPLACE CITY   COUNTY   STATE
23f. PRIOR NAME OF CHILD FIRST   MIDDLE   LAST   SUFFIX   23g. NEW NAME OF CHILD FIRST   MIDDLE   LAST   SUFFIX

CHILD 4
24a. FIRST NAME   MIDDLE   LAST   SUFFIX   24b. DATE OF BIRTH (mm/dd/yyyy)
24c. SOCIAL SECURITY NUMBER   24d. SEX   24e. BIRTHPLACE CITY   COUNTY   STATE
24f. PRIOR NAME OF CHILD FIRST   MIDDLE   LAST   SUFFIX   24g. NEW NAME OF CHILD FIRST   MIDDLE   LAST   SUFFIX

CONTINUED ON OTHER SIDE

WARNING: This is a governmental document. Texas Penal Code, Section 37.10, specifies penalties for making false entries or providing false information in this document.
VS-165 REV 6/98

TDH

Information on Suit
Affecting the Family Relationship

Back side

See text notes for filling out Section 4.

Leave this part blank.

Leave the rest blank

SECTION 4 (IF APPLICABLE)   OBLIGEE / OBLIGOR INFORMATION

OBLIGEE

THIS PARTY TO THE SUIT IS (CHECK ONE):
- ☐ 25a. TDPRS
- ☐ 25b. NON-PARENT CONSERVATOR - COMPLETE 26 - 32
- ☐ 25c. HUSBAND AS SHOWN ON FRONT OF THIS FORM - COMPLETE 31 - 32 ONLY
- ☐ 25d. WIFE AS SHOWN ON FRONT OF THIS FORM - COMPLETE 31 - 32 ONLY
- ☐ 25e. BIOLOGICAL FATHER - COMPLETE 26 - 32
- ☐ 25f. BIOLOGICAL MOTHER - COMPLETE 26 - 32

26. FIRST NAME   MIDDLE   LAST   SUFFIX   MAIDEN

27. DATE OF BIRTH (mm/dd/yyyy)   28. PLACE OF BIRTH   CITY   STATE OR FOREIGN COUNTRY

29. USUAL RESIDENCE   STREET NAME & NUMBER   CITY   COUNTY   STATE   ZIP

30. SOCIAL SECURITY NUMBER   31. DRIVER LICENSE NO & STATE   32. TELEPHONE NUMBER

OBLIGOR #1

THIS PARTY TO THE SUIT IS (CHECK ONE):
- ☐ 33a. NON-PARENT CONSERVATOR - COMPLETE 34 - 43
- ☐ 33b. HUSBAND AS SHOWN ON FRONT OF THIS FORM - COMPLETE 39 - 43 ONLY
- ☐ 33c. WIFE AS SHOWN ON FRONT OF THIS FORM - COMPLETE 39 - 43 ONLY
- ☐ 33d. BIOLOGICAL FATHER - COMPLETE 34 - 43
- ☐ 33e. BIOLOGICAL MOTHER - COMPLETE 34 - 43

34. FIRST NAME   MIDDLE   LAST   SUFFIX   MAIDEN

35. DATE OF BIRTH (mm/dd/yyyy)   36. PLACE OF BIRTH   CITY   STATE OR FOREIGN COUNTRY

37. USUAL RESIDENCE   STREET NAME & NUMBER   CITY   COUNTY   STATE   ZIP

38. SOCIAL SECURITY NUMBER   39. DRIVER LICENSE NO & STATE   40. TELEPHONE NUMBER

41. EMPLOYER NAME   42. EMPLOYER TELEPHONE NUMBER

43. EMPLOYER PAYROLL ADDRESS   STREET NAME & NUMBER   CITY   STATE   ZIP

OBLIGOR #2

THIS PARTY TO THE SUIT IS (CHECK ONE):
- ☐ 44a. NON-PARENT CONSERVATOR - COMPLETE 45 - 54
- ☐ 44b. HUSBAND AS SHOWN ON FRONT OF THIS FORM - COMPLETE 50 - 54 ONLY
- ☐ 44c. WIFE AS SHOWN ON FRONT OF THIS FORM - COMPLETE 50 - 54 ONLY
- ☐ 44d. BIOLOGICAL FATHER - COMPLETE 45 - 54
- ☐ 44e. BIOLOGICAL MOTHER - COMPLETE 45 - 54

45. FIRST NAME   MIDDLE   LAST   SUFFIX   MAIDEN

46. DATE OF BIRTH (mm/dd/yyyy)   47. PLACE OF BIRTH   CITY   STATE OR FOREIGN COUNTRY

48. USUAL RESIDENCE   STREET NAME & NUMBER   CITY   COUNTY   STATE   ZIP

49. SOCIAL SECURITY NUMBER   50. DRIVER LICENSE NO & STATE   51. TELEPHONE NUMBER

52. EMPLOYER NAME   53. EMPLOYER TELEPHONE NUMBER

54. EMPLOYER PAYROLL ADDRESS   STREET NAME & NUMBER   CITY   STATE   ZIP

SECTION 5 (IF APPLICABLE)   FOR ORDERS CONCERNING PATERNITY ESTABLISHMENT OF BIOLOGICAL FATHER

55. BIOLOGICAL FATHER'S NAME   FIRST   MIDDLE   LAST   SUFFIX   56. DATE OF BIRTH (mm/dd/yyyy)

57. SOCIAL SECURITY NUMBER   58. CURRENT MAILING ADDRESS   STREET NAME & NUMBER   CITY   STATE   ZIP

59. DOES THIS ORDER REMOVE INFORMATION PERTAINING TO A FATHER FROM A CHILD'S CERTIFICATE OF BIRTH? ☐ NO ☐ YES

SECTION 6   TERMINATION OF RIGHTS - Information related to the individual(s) whose rights are being terminated in this suit

60a. FIRST NAME   MIDDLE NAME   LAST NAME   SUFFIX   60b. RELATIONSHIP

61a. FIRST NAME   MIDDLE NAME   LAST NAME   SUFFIX   61b. RELATIONSHIP

62a. FIRST NAME   MIDDLE NAME   LAST NAME   SUFFIX   62b. RELATIONSHIP

Comments: _____

_____

I certify that the above order was granted on the date and place as stated.

_____
SIGNATURE OF THE CLERK OF THE COURT

9. The Statistics Form

10. The Hearing

In order to complete your divorce, and as the *last* (hooray!) item of business, you must attend a hearing and say a few words about your case. The hearing will be very brief, almost a mere formality. Most of your time will be spent waiting for it to start, and it will be over in a few minutes. So don't worry. In the next few pages, we show you how to set the date, what to do when you get there, and what to say. It is very unlikely that you will have any problems, but we have instructions to cover even that rare event.

A. Are You Ready? Prehearing Checklist

1. All cases

There is a 60-day waiting period, which is required in all cases. It can sometimes be quite tricky to compute, so it is safest to allow two months and two weeks to pass from the date you filed your Petition before the day of your hearing.

2. Waiver cases

If your spouse signed the Waiver form, and it is properly signed, notarized, and on file at the District Clerk's Office, then you can set the hearing as soon as the two-months-plus-two-weeks waiting period is over.

Make sure you have your Decree, the Withholding Order (if your Decree orders child support) and the Information on Suit Affecting Family Relationship form completed before you go in. If you plan to have your spouse's signature on the Decree or any other written agreements, this must be done before you go in for the hearing.

3. Default cases

Before you have your hearing:

a) at least two months plus two weeks must have passed since the date you filed your Petition, *and*

b) at least 27 days must have passed since the date your spouse was served with papers, *and*

c) at least 12 days must have passed since the date the Officer's Return (on the Citation) was filed with the District Clerk's Office.

B. Getting into Court

The way uncontested divorces are scheduled varies from county to county. It is usually informal, and always easy to do. When you are ready to set the date, call the District Clerk's Office and ask for the clerk of your court (give the number of the District Court that appears in the caption of your documents). Ask the clerk when uncontested divorce hearings are scheduled and also ask if they want any advance notice, either by phone or in writing, of when you will be coming in for your hearing.

Ask the clerk how the court's file for your case will get to the courtroom at the proper time. In some counties, you go into the District Clerk's Office ahead of the hearing and get your own file and carry it to the courtroom yourself. In other counties, you notify the clerk ahead of time when you are coming in for your hearing, and they send it to court for you.

We strongly recommend, some time before you have your own hearing, that you go into your courtroom as a spectator to watch other uncontested divorces. This will give you a very good idea of what will happen in your own case, and how your judge runs his or her courtroom. It will help you get ready for your own case. The Clerk's Office can tell you when uncontested divorces are heard by your court.

C. The Day of the Hearing

Get to the courthouse a little before your case is scheduled. Unless your county is one where the clerk does it for you, you should get your file from the District Clerk's Office, take it to your courtroom, and hand it to the bailiff (the guy with the uniform) or the clerk. Whether or not you are delivering a file, you should go up to the clerk or bailiff and let them know you are present and ready. Have a seat among the spectators and wait for your case to be called.

When your case is called, you answer "ready" and go up before the judge. The judge will administer the oath, then tell you to proceed. In some courts you stand before the judge's bench, and in others you will take the witness stand. The judge will indicate which you are to do. In either case, take time to arrange your papers and your notes, relax, and give your testimony. Always refer to the judge as "Your Honor" and don't lean on the bench if you are standing before it.

In some counties, a family law "master" or "referee" will hear the case. A master is a judge who is appointed by other judges, rather than elected. They have most of the duties of an elected judge, but their decisions must be approved by an elected judge. This will not be a problem for most people, especially if you have an agreed or default divorce. If the master asks you if you object to having him/her hear the case, say no. A master is called "Your Honor" just like an elected judge. If the master makes a ruling you disagree with, you have 3 days to ask an elected judge to review the master's decision.

If you are asked, state that you are willing to waive the presence of the court reporter. There is no particular advantage to having a word-for-word record of an uncontested divorce, and it is very expensive to make.

Your testimony will cover the basic facts of your case, the circumstances of your marriage, and what you are asking the court to do. It runs exactly parallel to your Petition, and what you ask for must match what is in your Decree.

The outline below is not exactly what you must say, but rather it is a guide to help you order your testimony. It is *not* a good idea to take this book into court and read from it, so you should type or write notes from these pages. Check off each item as you give it in court, and be sure you don't skip over or forget to say any part of it. Take your time, and relax. If the judge asks any questions, it is only because s/he is trying to become informed and be satisfied that justice, as s/he understands it, is being done. Don't worry, just answer, *briefly*, exactly the question asked. Don't volunteer information the judge does not ask for.

A Guide for Your Testimony

10. The Hearing

I. In every case, give the following information:

A. Your Honor, my name is _____, and I am the Petitioner in this case.

B. All of the facts stated in the Petition are true.

C. At the time of filing of this Petition, I had been continually a resident of Texas for more than six months, and of this county for more than 90 days.

D. I am now married to _____, who is the Respondent in this case. We were married on ____(date)_____, and we separated on ___(date) ____, and have not lived together as husband and wife since that time. (These dates must be the same as those given in the Petition. For common-law marriages, the language in the Petition is your guide for what to say at this point.)

E. I am seeking this divorce because our marriage has become insupportable due to discord or conflict of personalities, which has destroyed the legitimate ends of our marriage relationship. There is no chance for a reconciliation. Your Honor, I request that this marriage be dissolved. Would Your Honor like me to go into the particular circumstances of our marriage that led to this request for a divorce?

(If the judge says to do so, give a *brief* statement as to why your marriage cannot continue. Do not emphasize fault or blame, but describe differences, arguing, conflict, personality clashes, and so on. Tell about efforts to save the marriage. If there was any, describe violence, cruelty, drug abuse, abandonment, failure to support, neglect by your spouse. Conclude by stating that there is no possibility for a reconciliation.)

II. Continue, using the portions that apply to your case:

A. The Decree and Agreements:

Hand the Decree to the judge and state, "Your Honor, here is the Decree that I have prepared and that I am submitting to you at this time."

- If your spouse signed the Decree, state, "This Decree has been approved by my spouse, whose signature is on the last page. I am familiar with the signature of my spouse and can state that it is genuine."

- If there is a written agreement, hand the *original* and a copy to the judge at this time and state, "Here is the original and a copy of a written agreement between my spouse and myself. I am familiar with the signature of my spouse and can state that it is genuine. I request that the copy of the agreement be admitted into evidence and that the original be returned to me at the end of this hearing."

B. Children:

1) None:

Your Honor, my spouse and I have no minor, unmarried children, and none are expected.

2) If You Have Children:

If child custody and support are part of a written agreement, tell the judge: "The written agreement before your honor's consideration contains provisions concerning the custody and support of the child(ren)."

In every case, tell the court:

a) Your Honor, the Respondent and myself are the parents of (a) child(ren). (Give name, age, birthdate, and birthplace for each). Apart from personal possessions, no property is owned by the child(ren).

b) **Jurisdiction:** State one of the following:

- the Respondent is a resident of Texas, or

- the Respondent is not a resident of Texas, but: (State the best reasons that apply to your case from the list under "The parent/child long arm" in Chapter A, section 7.)

c) **Custody:** State one of the following:

- It would be in the best interest of the child(ren) for Respondent and I to be named Joint Managing Conservators.

- It would be in the best interest of the child(ren) if (I/Respondent) were to have the care, custody and control of the child(ren). The child(ren) live(s) with (me/Respondent) at this time, and (is/are) being well cared for. I am asking the court to name (me/my spouse) as Managing Conservator. (Be prepared to explain why this arrangement is better than Joint Managing Conservatorship.)

d) **Possession Schedule:**
Your Honor, it would be best for the children if the schedule for possession were to be ordered (state one of the following)

- (standard terms): for the specified times and places as set forth in the proposed Decree and the attached schedule, which is in substantial compliance with the Texas state standard for possession of minors.

- (major departure from the standard terms): for the specified times and places as set forth in the proposed Decree and the attached schedule. Your Honor, the reasons for requesting this particular schedule for possession are as follows (give reasons with any supporting evidence).

e) **Support:** Be prepared to testify to the income and earning ability of both spouses and the custodial parent's expenses. Optional: use the Financial Information form in the back of this book as a guide, take it to the hearing for reference, or submit it to the judge if he or she asks a lot of questions.

Your Honor, (I am/ my spouse is) able to earn a living and pay reasonable support for the child(ren). (State details or submit Financial Form.) I am requesting that (I/ my spouse) be ordered to pay (state terms you set out in Decree). I also request that the Court sign the attached Withholding Order.

f) **Class Attendance** (if required in your county):

- Your Honor, my spouse and I have completed the class required for parents. Here are the original certificates to be filed with the court.

  or

- Your Honor, I have completed the class required for parents. I have my certificate of completion to be filed with the court. I was unable to find my spouse to have him/her take the course. I request that you waive the requirement that my spouse take this class.

g) **Handicapped Child:** (Name of child) has a disability and requires continuous care and personal supervision and will not be capable of self-support. I request that payments for the support of this child be continued past the child's 18th birthday and extended for an indefinite period.

h) **Spousal Maintenance:** I am requesting that spousal maintenance be ordered. (State the qualifying grounds and the reason you need the support. Show him the Financial Form to back up your figures.)

C. Property and Debts:

1. **None:** Your Honor, there is no community property of any significant value apart from our personal effects.

2. **Approved Decree:** Your Honor, the Respondent and I have agreed to the division of property and debts as set forth in the Decree, and Respondent has signed the last page of that Decree. (Using your Petition as a guide, recite your community property and debts, and any separate property, then indicate which property and debts you wish the court to award to you and which to your spouse.)

3. **Written Contract:** The division of our community property and debts is covered by the written contract that I have submitted for Your Honor's approval. I request that you approve our agreement and incorporate it into the Decree.

4. **Divided by the Court:** Your Honor, there is some property in this case that should be fairly divided by order of this court.

   - During the marriage, we accumulated certain property, which is listed in the Petition. (Using your Petition as a guide, recite the property listed.)

   - There is also certain separate property, which is listed in the Petition, and which should be confirmed as separate property. (Recite the property, using the Petition as your guide.)

   - Your Honor, there are certain circumstances that make it fair that a large share of the property be awarded to (Petitioner/Respondent). (Recite the circumstances: custody of children requiring house and furniture, needs of one, earning ability of other, other circumstances, and so on.)

   - Your Honor, it is requested that the following division of property and debts be ordered: (Recite your request, following the terms of your prepared Decree.)

D. Change Of Name:

Your Honor, (I/Respondent) desire(s) and request(s) that (my/his/her) name be changed to ... (give desired name in full) ... (As of September 1, 1995, a judge can no longer refuse to change your name back to one you formerly used just because it would give you a different last name than your children.)

E. Conclusion:

State: "Your Honor, that concludes my testimony."

The judge may ask further questions, which you should answer briefly, sticking just to the point he asked about.

In almost all cases, the judge will announce the orders, sign your Decree, and you may go. You are finished. Divorced. It is over. Congratulations! Collect your papers, take all copies of the Decree to the clerk of your court, and get them stamped. Minor adjustments may be made by the clerk on the spot, but if the judge's orders were very different from your prepared Decree, you may have to make up a new Decree conforming exactly to the judge's orders, and present it for signing and stamping at a later time. Do it as soon as possible.

D. Troubleshooting Guide

We said it before and say it again: 99 times out of 100 there will be no trouble with the hearing. However, it will make you feel better if you know what to do just in case you are that unfortunate one.

1. Before the hearing begins

It sometimes happens that the people who work in the court forget who pays their salaries — that is, you and the other taxpayers. It usually does no good to remind them. Rather, if the clerk or the bailiff (or even the judge) is not helpful or polite, just keep calm, be polite, and firmly pursue your point. You have a right to represent yourself.

If someone is obstructing your way, it is very possible that there is a reason. If so, you must find it out and correct the problem. Ask what is the matter; at least get them to indicate the general area of the problem, or give you some hints as to the reason for their action or conduct. If necessary, ask to speak to another clerk, or to the supervisor. Don't get upset — the only important thing is for you to figure out and correct any errors in your papers or procedures. Go over this book and double-check everything. You can always come back to the Clerk's Office or to court another day.

2. After your hearing begins

This is a scary time for something to go wrong, but don't worry, you have an excellent escape hatch (or panic button) that you can use if all else fails. It is called the continuance. Lawyers use it all the time.

If things go very wrong and you can't figure out what your problem is, or how to solve it, or if you get into any kind of situation you can't handle, just tell the judge, "Your Honor, I respectfully request that this matter be continued to another date so that I may have time to seek advice and further prepare this case for presentation."

This way, you can come back another day, giving you time to try to find out what went wrong, or maybe ask to see the judge in chambers. Perhaps the judge will talk to you about it. It's worth a try. In any case, go over this book very carefully to see if you left anything out.

If the judge refuses to grant your divorce at the end of your testimony, this means he or she is not satisfied with some portion of it, that it is probably incomplete, something left out. Ask the judge, politely, to please explain his or her reasons, as it may be that you can give additional testimony that will solve the problem. If the judge indicates which portion of your case is incomplete, go over it again, more carefully and fully. If the judge will not help or explain, ask to have your case continued to another day. During the recess, see if the clerk or bailiff will help you, or ask to see the judge in chambers. Go over this book and double-check everything.

Assuming you find out what went wrong, go in for another hearing, and try it again.

3. After the hearing

If the judge grants your divorce but refuses to sign your Decree, then this probably means the judge thinks something is wrong with it. Probably it is different from the orders announced in court. The divorce is still valid and effective, but your case will not be over and complete until you can prepare a Decree that the judge will sign. Ask the judge what is wrong, and make careful note of the explanation. Ask the clerk. Look at the clerk's docket sheet (it's a public record) where notes are entered as to the orders in your case. Make up a new Decree and bring it in at another time, but do it as soon as possible.

Appendix

The Pauper's Oath

Rule 145 of the Texas Rules of Civil Procedure guarantees that no low-income Texan will be denied access to the courts simply because he or she cannot afford to pay the court costs. A party who is unable to afford costs is defined as *a person who is presently receiving a governmental entitlement based on indigency or any other person who has no ability to pay costs.*

Anyone receiving public assistance automatically qualifies under this rule.

The law does not contain guidelines for exactly how much income people not receiving public assistance can have and still qualify for the pauper's oath, but you would have to show that you can't pay for the essentials of life and also pay court fees. If you think you might qualify, go ahead and try it. The worst thing that can happen is they will decide you don't qualify.

Fill out the following two-page form, "Affidavit of Inability," as completely as possible, checking all applicable boxes. Sign it before a notary public and file it at the same time that you file your Petition.

PAUPER'S OATH

Cause No._____

IN THE MATTER OF THE MARRIAGE OF:

_____, Petitioner

AND

                                          IN THE DISTRICT COURT

_____, Respondent   OF _____ COUNTY

AND IN THE INTEREST OF   ___ JUDICIAL DISTRICT

_____

_____   CHILD(REN)

<u>AFFIDAVIT OF INABILITY</u>

THE STATE OF TEXAS)
)
COUNTY OF _____)

BEFORE ME, the undersigned authority, on this day personally appeared _____, who being by me duly sworn, on oath stated:

My name is _____. I am the Petitioner in the above referenced case. I believe that I have a meritorious claim. I verify that the statements made in this claim are true and correct.

I am unable to pay court costs for the following reasons.

I have approximately _____ in monthly expenses.

I have debts of approximately _____.

☐ I own no real estate, stocks, bonds or other property other than _____.

☐ I currently have _____ in cash.

☐ I am unemployed.

☐ My monthly income consists of _____ from the following sources _____

_____.

☐ I have no other income.

☐ I do not have access to any income from my spouse.

Signed: _____
                                    PLAINTIFF

SUBSCRIBED AND SWORN TO BEFORE ME
on this _____ day of _____, 20___.

_____
                            NOTARY PUBLIC, STATE OF TEXAS

The Forms

Order of the Forms

Original Petition for Divorce

Waiver of Citation

Citation (within county)

Citation (outside county)

Information for Service of Process

Decree of Divorce

*Order/Notice to Withhold Income for Child Support

*Employer's Order to Withhold Earnings for Spousal Maintenance

*Request to Issue Withholding Order

*Financial Information

*Standard Schedule for Possession

*Information on Suit Affecting the Family Relationship

Power of Attorney to Transfer Motor Vehicle

Special Warranty Deed (to Transfer Real Property)

*These are used only if you have children

Cause No._____

IN THE MATTER OF THE MARRIAGE OF:

_____, Petitioner

AND

IN THE DISTRICT COURT

OF _____ COUNTY

_____, Respondent

___ JUDICIAL DISTRICT

AND IN THE INTEREST OF

_____

_____ CHILD(REN)

ORIGINAL PETITION FOR DIVORCE

...Discovery Level 1 applies to this case as there are no minor children of the marriage whose custody and support will be determined AND the value of the marital estate is between zero and $50,000.00.

...Discovery Level 2 applies to this case as there are minor children of the marriage whose custody and support will be determined AND/OR the value of the marital estate is more than $50,000.00.

This suit is brought by _____

Petitioner, Soc.Sec.#_____, Driver's License #_____

age _____, who resides at _____

Respondent is _____

Soc.Sec.#_____, Driver's License #_____ age _____

who resides at _____

I. RESIDENCY:

Petitioner has been a domiciliary of the State of Texas for the preceding six months and a resident of the county in which this petition is filed for the preceding ninety days.

....Respondent is a domiciliary of the State of Texas.

....Long Arm: Respondent is a nonresident of Texas.

II. SERVICE OF PROCESS:

...Waiver: No service is necessary at this time.

...Process should be served on Respondent at

_____

_____

III. MARRIAGE:

...Petitioner and Respondent were married on or about
_____, ____, and lived together as husband and wife
until on or about _____, ____, at which time they
separated and ceased to live together.

...Common-Law Marriage: Petitioner and Respondent agreed to be
married on or about _____, ____, and thereafter lived
together in Texas as husband and wife and there represented to others
that they were married, thus creating a common-law marriage. The parties
separated on or about _____, _____.

IV. GROUNDS:

The marriage has become insupportable because of discord or
conflict of personalities that destroys the legitimate ends of the
marriage relationship and prevents any reasonable expectation of
reconciliation.

V. PROPERTY (INCLUDES DEBTS):

...No property: To Petitioner's knowledge, there is no community
property of any significant value other than personal effects which is
subject to division by the court at this time.

...Divided by agreement: Petitioner believes the parties will
reach an agreed property division and ask the Court to approve that
agreement when presented to the Court.

...Marital Settlement Contract: The parties have entered into
a Marital Settlement Contract, a copy of which is attached and
incorporated by reference.

...Divided by Court:
(1) Itemization: To Petitioner's knowledge, the property of
the parties consists of the following described items:

        (2) Division: Petitioner requests the Court to order a division of the property in a manner that the Court deems just and right, as provided by law.

        ...It would be fair for the property to be divided into approximately equal portions.

        ...There are many equities which the court should consider making it fair that_____be awarded a substantial portion of the property.

        ...It will be fair and equitable for the Court to award as Petitioner's separate property the property described in the above list at items numbered:

        It will be fair and equitable for the Court to order Respondent to assume and to pay without any right to contribution or reimbursement from Petitioner the debts described in the above list at items numbered:

VI. SPOUSAL MAINTENANCE:

...Maintenance is not requested.

...Petitioner requests that this court award maintenance for the following reasons:

...Petitioner and Respondent were married at least 10 years

...Respondent was convicted of or received deferred adjudication for a family violence crime within two years from the date of the filing of this Petition

and Petitioner lacks sufficient property, including property distributed after this divorce, to provide for Petitioner's minimum reasonable needs; and Petitioner

...clearly lacks the earning ability in the labor market adequate to provide for Petitioner's minimum reasonable needs.

...is unable to support him/herself through employment because of an incapacitating physical or mental disability.

...is the custodian of a child who requires substantial care and personal supervision because of a physical or mental disability which makes it necessary that Petitioner not be employed outside of the home.

VII. CHANGE OF NAME:

It is requested that the Court order a change of name for _____

_____ and that the name be changed to:

VIII. CHILDREN:

...No unmarried children now under eighteen years of age were born to or adopted by the parties of the marriage and none is expected.

...The following child(ren) now under eighteen years old were born to or adopted by the parties of the marriage:

Name	Age	Sex	Birthdate	Birthplace
1.				
2.				
3.				
4.				
5.				

These children reside at:

No other person is entitled to notice of this suit. No court ordered relationship exists between the child(ren) and any other person. No other court has continuing, exclusive jurisdiction over any child in the above list.

No property, apart from personal effects, is owned by the child(ren) in the above list, except as listed here:

..._____, a child of this marriage, requires continuous care and personal supervision because of a disability and will not be capable of self-support. The Court is requested to order that payments for the support of this child be continued after the child's eighteenth birthday and extended for an indefinite period.

...Respondent is not a resident of Texas, but this court may exercise personal jurisdiction over him because:

...The above child(ren) (was/were) conceived in Texas and Respondent is a parent.

...Respondent resided in Texas and provided prenatal expenses and/or support for the child(ren).

...Respondent resided with the child(ren) in Texas

...The child(ren) reside(s) in Texas as a result of the acts or directives or with the approval of the Respondent.

...Private health care coverage is currently in effect for the child(ren) and _____ is responsible for paying the premium of _____ per month. Said insurance, (provided / not provided) through the payor's employment, is via the following policy:

...There is currently no private health care coverage in effect for the child(ren) and

...the child(ren) is/are not receiving health care under any public health care program.

...the child(ren) is/are receiving health care under the following public health care program(s):

IX. CONSERVATORSHIP AND SUPPORT:

Upon final hearing,

...Petitioner and Respondent should be appointed Joint Managing Conservators of the child(ren) and _____ should have the right to establish the primary residence of the child(ren).

..._____ should be appointed the Sole Managing Conservator of the child(ren) and _____ should be appointed Possessory Conservator of the child(ren).

_____ should be ordered to make payments for the support of the children in the manner specified by the Court. Possession should be arranged according to the best interests of the child(ren).

X. PROTECTIVE ORDERS:

... There is no protective order between the parties.

... A protective order is presently in effect or an application for protective order is pending at this time. A true and correct copy of the protective order
        ... is attached to this Original Petition.
        ... is unavailable at this time but will be filed with the court before any hearings in this case.

STATEMENT OF ALTERNATIVE DISPUTE RESOLUTION

I AM AWARE THAT IT IS THE POLICY OF THE STATE OF TEXAS TO PROMOTE THE AMICABLE AND NONJUDICIAL SETTLEMENT OF DISPUTES INVOLVING CHILDREN AND FAMILIES. I AM AWARE OF ALTERNATIVE DISPUTE RESOLUTION METHODS INCLUDING MEDIATION. WHILE I RECOGNIZE THAT ALTERNATIVE DISPUTE RESOLUTION IS AN ALTERNATIVE TO AND NOT A SUBSTITUTE FOR A TRIAL AND THAT THIS CASE MAY BE TRIED IF IT IS NOT SETTLED, I REPRESENT TO THE COURT THAT I WILL ATTEMPT IN GOOD FAITH TO RESOLVE BEFORE FINAL TRIAL CONTESTED ISSUES IN THIS CASE BY ALTERNATIVE DISPUTE RESOLUTION WITHOUT THE NECESSITY OF COURT INTERVENTION.

PRAYER

...Petitioner prays that citation and notice issue as required by law.

Petitioner prays that the Court grant a divorce and decree such other relief as is requested in this petition.

Petitioner prays for such other and further relief, general and special, to which Petitioner may be entitled.

Dated: _____, 20___.

_____, Pro Se
                    Petitioner

Address _____

_____

Phone: _____

Cause No. _____

IN THE MATTER OF THE MARRIAGE OF:

_____, Petitioner

AND

_____, Respondent

AND IN THE INTEREST OF

_____

_____CHILD(REN)

IN THE DISTRICT COURT

OF _____COUNTY

___ JUDICIAL DISTRICT

WAIVER OF CITATION

THE STATE OF _____

COUNTY OF _____

BEFORE ME, the undersigned authority, on this day personally appeared _____ who, being by me duly sworn, upon oath says:

My name is _____
Social Security #_____ Driver's License # _____
My address is _____

_____

I am the Respondent in the above entitled and numbered cause. I have received a copy of the Original Petition which I have read and understand.

I hereby enter my appearance in said cause for all purposes, waive the issuance, service and return of citation upon me, and agree that said cause may be taken up and considered by the Court at any time without further notice to me. I agree that this case may be heard by a duly appointed master or referee of this court. I waive the making of a record of testimony.

Further, I hereby waive all rights and privileges, including appointment of counsel, pursuant to the Soldier's and Sailor's Civil Relief Act of 1940.

I AM AWARE THAT IT IS THE POLICY OF THE STATE OF TEXAS TO PROMOTE THE AMICABLE AND NONJUDICIAL SETTLEMENT OF DISPUTES INVOLVING CHILDREN AND FAMILIES. I AM AWARE OF ALTERNATIVE DISPUTE RESOLUTION METHODS INCLUDING MEDIATION. WHILE I RECOGNIZE THAT ALTERNATIVE DISPUTE RESOLUTION IS AN ALTERNATIVE TO AND NOT A SUBSTITUTE FOR A TRIAL AND THAT THIS CASE MAY BE TRIED IF IT IS NOT SETTLED, I PREPRESENT TO THE COURT THAT I WILL ATTEMPT IN GOOD FAITH TO RESOLVE BEFORE FINAL TRIAL CONTESTED ISSUES IN THIS CASE BY ALTERNATIVE DISPUTE RESOLUTION WITHOUT THE NECESSITY OF COURT INTERVENTION.

/s/ _____
                        Respondent

SWORN TO AND SUBSCRIBED BEFORE ME by the said

_____on this _____ day of _____, 20____, to certify which witness my hand and seal of office.

/s/ _____
                        NOTARY PUBLIC

THE STATE OF TEXAS   (Respondent Within the County)

Notice to Defendant: You have been sued. You may employ an attorney. If you or your attorney do not file a written answer with the clerk who issued this citation by 10:00 a.m. on the Monday next following the expiration of twenty days after you were served this citation and petition, a default judgment may be taken against you.

TO: _____ Defendant, Greeting:

You are hereby commanded to appear by filing a written answer to the Plaintiff's Petition at or before ten o'clock a.m. of the Monday next after the expiration of twenty days after the date of service of this citation before the ____ District Court of _____ County, Texas, at the courthouse of said County in the City of _____, Texas.

Said Plaintiff's Petition was filed in said court on the ____ day of _____, 20___, in this case, numbered _____, and styled

_____, Petitioner, and _____, Respondent.

The nature of Petitioner's demand is fully shown by a true and correct copy of the Petition accompanying this citation and made a part hereof.

The officer executing this writ shall promptly serve the same according to requirements of law, and the mandates thereof, and make due return as the law directs. Issued and given under my hand and seal of said Court at _____, Texas, this ____ day of _____, 20___,

Attest: _____

Clerk, District Court, _____ County, Texas

By _____, Deputy.

OFFICER'S RETURN

The within citation came to hand on the ____ day of _____. 20___, at _____ o'clock (am)(pm), and was by me executed at _____, within the county of _____, at _____ o'clock (am)(pm), on the ____ day of _____, 20___, by delivering to the within named _____ in person, a true copy of this citation, having first endorsed thereon the date of delivery, together with the accompanying true and correct copy of the Petition.

Sheriff's Fee............ $_____

| **Sheriff Account** |
| No. _____ |

To certify which witness my hand officially: _____

_____

Sheriff of _____ County, Texas

By _____, Deputy

| **For Clerk's Use** |
| Taxed _____ |
| Return recorded _____ |

THE STATE OF TEXAS   (Respondent Without the County)

Notice to Defendant: You have been sued. You may employ an attorney. If you or your attorney do not file a written answer with the clerk who issued this citation by 10:00 a.m. on the Monday next following the expiration of twenty days after you were served this citation and petition, a default judgment may be taken against you.

TO: _____ Defendant, Greeting:

You are hereby commanded to appear by filing a written answer to the Plaintiff's Petition at or before ten o'clock a.m. of the Monday next after the expiration of twenty days after the date of service of this citation before the ____ District Court of _____ County, Texas, at the courthouse of said County in the City of _____, Texas.

Said Plaintiff's Petition was filed in said court on the ____ day of _____, 20___, in this case, numbered _____, and styled

_____, Petitioner, and _____, Respondent.

The nature of Petitioner's demand is fully shown by a true and correct copy of the Petition accompanying this citation and made a part hereof.

The officer executing this writ shall promptly serve the same according to requirements of law, and the mandates thereof, and make due return as the law directs. Issued and given under my hand and seal of said Court at _____ , Texas, this _____ day of _____, 20___,

Attest: _____

Clerk, District Court, _____ County, Texas

By _____ , Deputy.

RETURN

The State of_____
County of _____

Before me, the undersigned authority, on this day personally appeared _____ _____ , a person not interested in the within-mentioned suit, above 21 years of age, of sound mind and competent to make oath, and being sworn, deposed and said:

My name is _____; I am disinterested in the within styled and numbered cause, above 21 years of age, of sound mind and competent to make oath of the facts below:

The within citation came to hand on the _____ day of _____, 20___, at _____ o'clock (am)(pm), and was by me executed at _____ within the county of _____ ,at _____ o'clock (am)(pm), on the ____ day of _____, 20___, by delivering to the within named _____ in person, a true copy of this citation, having first endorsed thereon the date of delivery, together with the accompanying true and correct copy of the Petition.

The distance actually travelled by me in serving such process was _____ miles, and my fees are as follows: For serving this citation...... $ _____

For mileage	$ _____	
For notary	$ _____	
Total fees	$ _____	

Sheriff Account	
No. _____	

To certify which witness my hand officially: _____
Signed and sworn to by the said _____ , before me this _____ day of _____, 20___, to certify which witness my hand and seal of office.

For Clerk's Use
Taxed _____
Return recorded _____

_____

Notary Public, _____ County,

_____ . (or other competent officer.)

INFORMATION FOR SERVICE OF PROCESS

FROM: _____

      Address_____

      _____

      Phone(s)_____

TO: _____

       _____

       _____

       RE: In the Matter of the Marriage of:

       _____, Petitioner,

       and _____, Respondent.

               Cause No. _____

               In the _____ District Court of

               _____County, Texas

Dear Sir:

Enclosed are copies of a Petition and Citation, and a money order for $_____.

The enclosed papers MUST be served within 90 days of the date of issuance of the Citation in order to be valid. The Return portion of the Citation must, of course, be completely and accurately filled out and signed.

NOTE TO OFFICERS OUTSIDE THE STATE OF TEXAS:
The signature of the officer delivering the Citation and Petition MUST be sworn and Notarized in order to be effective in Texas.

INFORMATION FOR SERVICE OF PROCESS:

Person to Be Served: _____

Address: Residence: _____

               _____

          Work: _____

          Other: _____

Physical Description: _____

_____

COMMENTS:

Cause No. _____

IN THE MATTER OF THE MARRIAGE OF:

_____, Petitioner

AND

_____, Respondent

IN THE DISTRICT COURT

OF _____ COUNTY

____ JUDICIAL DISTRICT

AND IN THE INTEREST OF

_____

_____CHILD(REN)

DECREE OF DIVORCE

On the _____ day of _____, 20___, final hearing was held in this cause.

Petitioner, _____, Soc.Sec.#_____, Driver's License #,appeared in person, pro se, and announced ready for trial.

Respondent, _____, Soc.Sec.#_____, Driver's License #_____.

...was duly and properly cited by personal service and failed to appear.

...waived issuance and service of citation by waiver duly filed and did not otherwise appear.

The making of a record of testimony was waived by the parties with consent of the Court.

Because a jury was not demanded by either party, the Court tried the cause.

The Court, having examined the pleadings and heard the evidence finds that all necessary residence requirements and prerequisites of law have been legally satisfied; that this Court has personal jurisdiction of the parties and of the subject matter of this cause; and that the material allegations of the petition are true.

DIVORCE DECREE

THE COURT FINDS that Petitioner and Respondent were married, and that their marriage had become insupportable because of discord or conflict of personalities which destroyed the legitimate ends of the marriage without any reasonable expectation of reconciliation.

THE COURT ORDERS AND DECREES that the marriage of Petitioner and Respondent is dissolved and that they are hereby divorced.

EMPLOYEE RETIREMENT BENEFITS

THE COURT FINDS with respect to employee retirement benefits:

...That there is no community interest in any retirement plan or other benefit program existing by reason of either party's past or present employment that is subject to division by the Court at this time.

...THE COURT FINDS that _____ is a participant in a retirement program known as_____ _____, as to which the Court reserves jurisdiction to adjudicate the respective rights of the parties at a future date upon application of either party. IT IS HEREBY ORDERED that _____ shall not apply for or accept benefits under said program without prior written notice to _____ _____ and application to this Court for determination and division of community rights in said plan. IT IS ORDERED that any party requesting a division or clarification of retirement shall do so within two (2) years of the date this decree is signed by the court, or the party shall lose that right.

SEPARATE PROPERTY

...THE COURT FINDS THAT there is no property to be confirmed as the separate property of either party.

...THE COURT FINDS THAT certain property was and is the separate property of the Petitioner, and IT IS HEREBY ORDERED AND DECREED that the following property is confirmed as Petitioner's sole and separate property:

PROPERTY DIVISION

...THE COURT FINDS THAT the parties do not own any community property of any significant value other than their personal effects.

THE COURT ORDERS AND DECREES that each party is awarded the personal effects presently in their possession as his or her separate property.

...THE COURT FINDS THAT the parties have entered into a written agreement for the division of their property and debts and that the agreement is just and right.

THE COURT ORDERS AND DECREES that the agreement of the parties, which is attached here as Exhibit "A" and incorporated herein for all purposes, be and is approved.

...THE COURT FINDS THAT the parties possess certain community property and debts which should be justly divided.

THE COURT ORDERS AND DECREES that the estate of the parties is divided as follows:

(1) The following property and debts are hereby awarded as Petitioner's sole and separate property, and Respondent is divested of all right, title, and interest in and to said property:

(2) The following property and debts are hereby awarded as Respondent's sole and separate property, and Petitioner is divested of all right, title, and interest in and to said property:

IT IS FURTHER ORDERED AND DECREED that the party awarded a debt shall indemnify and hold harmless the other party from any failure to discharge such debt.

INCOME TAXES

IT IS ORDERED that Petitioner and Respondent shall each be responsible for all taxes attributable to their own income only and each entitled to their own refunds for the year of the divorce.

IT IS FURTHER ORDERED that Petitioner shall pay _____ percent and Respondent shall pay _____ percent of any income tax liability acrued prior to the year of the divorce, and that Petitioner shall receive _____ percent and Respondent shall receive _____ percent of any income tax refund accrued prior to the year of the divorce.

MAINTENANCE

The Court finds maintenance should be awarded on the following grounds:

...Petitioner and Respondent were married at least ten (10) years.

...Respondent was convicted of or received deferred adjudication for a family violence crime within two years from the date of the filing of this Petition.

and Petitioner lacks sufficient property, including property distributed after this divorce, to provide for Petitioner's minimum reasonable needs; and Petitioner

...clearly lacks the earning ability in the labor market adequate to provide for Petitioner's minimum reasonable needs.

...is unable to support him/herself through employment because of an incapacitating physical or mental disability.

...is the custodian of a child who requires substantial care and personal supervision because of a physcal or mental disability which makes it necessary that Petitioner not be employed outside of the home.

THEREFORE, IT IS ORDERED _____ (paying party) pay to _____ (receiving party) for spousal maintenance the sum of $_____ per month, due and payable beginning _____, 20____ and continuing on the same day of each month thereafter until

either party dies; or
the receiving party remarries. This order for maintenance shall continue for

... for _____ months not to exceed thirty six (36) months.

... for an indefinite period.

IT IS FURTHER ORDERED that all payments shall be made by _____ (paying party) to _____ (receiving party) at any address designated in writing by _____ (receiving party).

CHILDREN

...THE COURT FINDS that there is no unmarried child of the marriage under eighteen years of age and none is expected.

THE COURT FINDS that the following unmarried children under the age of eighteen were born to or adopted by the parties to the marriage and that no other is expected:

Name:_____ Sex:___ Age:____ Birthdate: _____
Present residence: _____
Birthplace: _____ SSN_____ DL #_____

Name:_____ Sex:___ Age:____ Birthdate: _____
Present residence: _____
Birthplace: _____ SSN_____ DL #_____

Name:_____ Sex:___ Age:____ Birthdate: _____
Present residence: _____
Birthplace: _____ SSN_____ DL #_____

Name:_____ Sex:___ Age:____ Birthdate: _____
Present residence: _____
Birthplace: _____ SSN_____ DL #_____

Name:_____ Sex:___ Age:____ Birthdate: _____
Present residence: _____
Birthplace: _____ SSN_____ DL #_____

THE COURT FINDS that the children do not own or possess any property other than their personal effects.

CONSERVATORSHIP

...THE COURT FINDS that the parties have made a written agreement concerning conservatorship of the child(ren) and that it is in the child(ren)'s best interest.

THE COURT FINDS, after considering the circumstances, that the following orders are in the best interest of the child(ren):

THE COURT ORDERS AND DECREES that

..._____ and _____
are appointed Joint Managing Conservators of the child(ren)

..._____ is appointed the Sole Managing Conservator of the child(ren) and _____ is appointed Possessory Conservator of the child(ren)

with all the rights and duties of a parent at all times, including: the right to receive information from the other parent concerning the health, education and welfare of the child(ren); to confer with the other parent to the extent possible before making decisions concerning the health, education and welfare of the child(ren); of access to medical, dental, psychological and educational records of the child(ren); to consult with a physician, dentist or psychologist of the child(ren); to consult with school officials concerning the child(ren); to consult with school officials concerning the child(ren)'s welfare and educational status, including school activities; to be designated on the

child's records as a person to be notified in case of an emergency; to consent to medical, dental and surgical treatment during an emergency involving an immediate danger to the health and safety of the child; to inherit from and through the child(ren); and to manage the estate of the child(ren) to the extent the estate was created by the parent or the parent's family.

THE COURT ORDERS AND DECREES that _____ and _____, shall each have the following rights and duties during the period each has possession of the child(ren): the duty of care, control, protection and reasonable discipline of the child(ren); the duty to support the child(ren), including providing clothing, food, shelter and medical and dental care not involving an invasive procedure; the right to consent for the child(ren) to medical and dental care not involving an invasive procedure; the right to consent for the child(ren) to medical, dental and surgical treatment during an emergency involving immediate danger to the health and safety of the child(ren); and the right to direct the moral and religious training of the child(ren).

THE COURT ORDERS AND DECREES that each parent has a duty to inform the other parent in a timely manner of significant information concerning the health, education and welfare of the child(ren).

....THE COURT ORDERS AND DECREES that _____ shall have the right to establish the primary residence (domicile) of the children.

....THE COURT ORDERS AND DECREES that the residence of the child(ren) shall remain in _____ County and any contiguous county thereto until further order of the Court.

....THE COURT ORDERS AND DECREES the child(ren)'s primary residence may be established by _____ without restriction.

THE COURT FURTHER ORDERS AND DECREES that each party as named below shall have the following rights and duties exclusively:

_____ shall have the right to consent to medical, dental and surgical treatment involving invasive procedures, and to consent to psychiatric and psychological treatment;

_____ shall have the right to receive and give receipt for periodic payments for the support of the child(ren) (child support) and to hold or disburse these funds for the benefit of the child(ren);

_____ shall have the right to represent the child(ren) in legal action and to make other decisions of substantial legal significance concerning the child(ren);

_____ shall have the right to make decisions concerning the child(ren)'s education;

_____ shall have the right to the services and earnings of the child(ren); and

except when a guardian of the child(ren)'s estate or guardian or attorney at litem has been appointed for the child(ren), _____ _____ shall have the right to act as an agent of the child(ren) in relation to the child(ren)'s estate if the child(ren)'s action is required by a state, the United States or a foreign government.

THE COURT ORDERS AND DECREES that _____ shall have the right to visit with and temporarily take possession of the child(ren):

...at the specific times and places specified below:

...at such specific times and places as are set forth in the attached Schedule for Possession of Minor Children which is incorporated herein for all purposes by this reference. This schedule shall take effect on that child's third birthday, and, until such time, the schedule shall be:

...at the specific times and places set forth below:

...at the specific times and places set forth in the attached Schedule for Possession of Children Under Three Years which is incorporated herein for all purposes by this reference. For purposes of this Standard Possession Order, the (choose one) Joint/Possessory Conservator having temporary possession shall be called "Possessory Conservator" or "PC" and the parent who regularly has possession of the children shall be called "Managing Conservator" or "MC." IT IS ORDERED that these terms, as used in the Standard Possession Order, do not change any rights or duties of a parent assigned to that parent in the above court order.

_____ (parent receiving temporary possession) IS ORDERED not to interfere with the Conservatorship of the child(ren) and to return the child(ren) to the care of _____ _____ (other parent) immediately upon the termination of each ordered or agreed period of possession.

_____ (parent child(ren) usually reside with) IS ORDERED to surrender the child(ren) to _____ _____ (parent receiving temporary possession) at the beginning of each ordered or agreed period of possession.

CHILD SUPPORT

THE COURT FINDS that _____ is capable of gainful employment and is able to contribute to the support of the child(ren). THE COURT FINDS that the monthly net resources of _____ _____ are _____.

THE COURT ORDERS AND DECREES that _____,
hereafter Obligor, is obligated to pay and, subject to the income
withholding provisions specified below, shall pay to _____
_____, hereafter Obligee, child support in the total amount of
$_____ per month, payable beginning on the _____ day of
_____, 20___, and a like payment being due and payable on the
same day of each subsequent month, continuing thereafter until the
earliest of any of the following conditions occur for any child:

1) the child reaches the age of 18 years, and thereafter, so long
   as the child is fully enrolled in an accredited primary or
   secondary school in a program leading toward a high school
   diploma, until the end of the school term in which the child
   graduates;
2) the child marries;
3) the child dies;
4) the child's disabilities are otherwise removed for general
   purposes;
5) the child is otherwise emancipated; or
6) until further order of the court.

Thereafter, Obligor is ORDERED AND DECREED to pay to Obligee child
support of $_____ per month, with the first payment being due and
payable on the _____ day of each month until the first month following the
date of the next occurrence of one of the events specified above.

...THE COURT FINDS THAT _____ is a child
in need of support as defined in section 154.302 of the Texas Family
Code, and therefore THE COURT ORDERS AND DECREES that of the above
amount ordered for child support, and notwithstanding any other language
above, the amount of $_____ per month for the support of said child
shall be a continuing obligation until further order of the Court.

IT IS FURTHER ORDERED that for the term of the child support
obligation for each child,

...as additional child support, Obligor shall carry and maintain
medical health insurance for the benefit of said child.

...Obligee shall carry and maintain medical health coverage
for the benefit of said child.

...Obligor will reimburse Obligee for amounts Obligee pays
for medical health coverage for said child, and that amount has been
included in the child support figure above.

IT IS FURTHER ORDERED that Obligor shall pay ____ percent and
Obligee shall pay ____ percent of the child(ren)'s medical expenses that
are not reimbursed by insurance.

IT IS FURTHER ORDERED that for the term of the child support obligation, the parties shall keep each other informed of mailing address, residence address and telephone number, name of employer, address of employment and work telephone number, or status of employment. Each party who intends changing place of residence must give written notice of the intended date of change, new telephone number and new street address of residence to the other party 60 days before such change. If the party did not know of the change within the 60 day period, notice must be given within 5 days after the party knew or should have known of the change. This notice may be served by delivery of a copy of the notice to the party to be served either in person or by registered or certified mail, return receipt requested, to the last known address of the party to be served.

FAILURE TO OBEY A COURT ORDER FOR CHILD SUPPORT OR FOR POSSESSION OF OR ACCESS TO A CHILD MAY RESULT IN FURTHER LITIGATION TO ENFORCE THE ORDER, INCLUDING CONTEMPT OF COURT. A FINDING OF CONTEMPT MAY BE PUNISHED BY A CONFINEMENT IN JAIL FOR UP TO SIX MONTHS, A FINE OF UP TO $500 FOR EACH VIOLATION, AND A MONEY JUDGMENT FOR PAYMENT OF ATTORNEY'S FEES AND COURT COSTS.

FAILURE OF A PARTY TO MAKE A CHILD SUPPORT PAYMENT TO THE PLACE AND IN THE MANNER REQUIRED BY A COURT ORDER MAY RESULT IN THE PARTY NOT RECEIVING CREDIT FOR MAKING THE PAYMENT.

FAILURE OF A PARTY TO PAY CHILD SUPPORT DOES NOT JUSTIFY DENYING THAT PARTY COURT-ORDERED POSSESSION OF OR ACCESS TO A CHILD. REFUSAL BY A PARTY TO ALLOW POSSESSION OF OR ACCESS TO A CHILD DOES NOT JUSTIFY FAILURE TO PAY COURT-ORDERED CHILD SUPPORT TO THAT PARTY.

EACH PERSON WHO IS A PARTY TO THIS ORDER OR DECREE IS ORDERED TO NOTIFY EACH OTHER PARTY, THE CLERK OF THIS COURT, AND THE STATE CASE REGISTRY OF ANY CHANGE IN THE PARTY'S CURRENT RESIDENCE ADDRESS, MAILING ADDRESS, HOME TELEPHONE NUMBER, DRIVER'S LICENSE NUMBER, NAME OF EMPLOYER, ADDRESS OF EMPLOYMENT, AND WORK TELEPHONE NUMBER. THE PARTY IS ORDERED TO GIVE NOTICE OF AN INTENDED CHANGE IN ANY OF THE REQUIRED INFORMATION TO EACH OTHER PARTY, THE COURT AND THE STATE CASE REGISTRY ON OR BEFORE THE 60TH DAY BEFORE THE INTENDED CHANGE. IF THE PARTY DOES NOT KNOW OR COULD NOT HAVE KNOWN OF THE CHANGE IN SUFFICIENT TIME TO PROVIDE 60-DAY NOTICE, THE PARTY IS ORDERED TO GIVE NOTICE OF THE CHANGE ON OR BEFORE THE FIFTH DAY AFTER THE DATE THAT THE PARTY KNOWS OF THE CHANGE.

THE DUTY TO FURNISH THIS INFORMATION TO EACH OTHER PARTY, THE COURT AND THE STATE CASE REGISTRY CONTINUES AS LONG AS ANY PERSON, BY VIRTUE OF THIS ORDER, IS UNDER AN OBLIGATION TO PAY CHILD SUPPORT OR ENTITLED TO POSSESSION OF OR ACCESS TO A CHILD.

FAILURE BY A PARTY TO OBEY THE ORDER OF THIS COURT TO PROVIDE EACH OTHER PARTY, THE COURT AND THE STATE CASE REGISTRY WITH THE CHANGE IN THE REQUIRED INFORMATION MAY RESULT IN FURTHER LITIGATION TO ENFORCE THE ORDER, INCLUDING CONTEMPT OF COURT. A FINDING OF CONTEMPT MAY BE PUNISHED BY CONFINEMENT IN JAIL FOR UP TO SIX MONTHS, A FINE OF UP TO $500 FOR EACH VIOLATION, AND A MONEY JUDGMENT FOR PAYMENT OF ATTORNEY'S FEES AND COURT COSTS.

INCOME WITHHOLDING AND PAYMENT OF SUPPORT

THE COURT ORDERS AND DECREES that the above child support obligation shall be discharged, pro tanto, by income withholding. The attached "Employer's Order To Withhold Earnings," which was signed by the Court on this date, is wholly incorporated herein for all purposes by reference, and any employer of Obligor IS ORDERED to withhold income according to the terms set forth therein or until further order of the Court.

IT IS FURTHER ORDERED that Obligor is ordered to claim no fewer than the actual number of his/her dependents on the W-4 form.

IT IS FURTHER ORDERED that all amounts withheld and paid in accordance with said order shall constitute a credit against the child support obligation. If the amount so withheld and paid is less than 100% of the amount ordered to be paid by this decree, the balance due remains an obligation of Obligor, and it IS ORDERED that Obligor pay the balance due directly to the registry, office, or person specified below.

IT IS ORDERED that all payments for child support be made through:

and then promptly remitted to the party receiving child support for the support of the children.

IT IS ORDERED that, upon request of a prosecuting attorney, the Attorney General, the Obligee or the Obligor, the clerk of this Court shall cause a certified copy of the "Employer's Order To Withhold Earnings" to be delivered to any employer. IT IS FURTHER ORDERED that the clerk of this Court shall attach a copy of Chapter 158, Subchapter C of the Texas Family Code for the information of any employer.

INFORMATION REGARDING PARTIES AND CHILD(REN)

     The information required for each party by section 105.006(a) of the Texas Family Code is as follows:

Name: _____
     Social Security number: _____
     Driver's license number: _____ Issuing state:_____
     Current residence address: _____
          _____
     Mailing address: _____
     Home telephone number: _____
     Name of employer: _____
     Address of employment: _____
     Work telephone number: _____

Name: _____
     Social Security number: _____
     Driver's license number: _____ Issuing state:_____
     Current residence address: _____
          _____
     Mailing address: _____
     Home telephone number: _____
     Name of employer: _____
     Address of employment: _____
     Work telephone number: _____

Name: _____
     Social Security number: _____
     Driver's license number: _____ Issuing state:_____
     Current residence address: _____
          _____
     Mailing address: _____
     Home telephone number: _____
     Name of employer: _____
     Address of employment: _____
     Work telephone number: _____

Name: _____
     Social Security number: _____
     Driver's license number: _____ Issuing state:_____
     Current residence address: _____
          _____
     Mailing address: _____
     Home telephone number: _____
     Name of employer: _____
     Address of employment: _____
     Work telephone number: _____

...IT IS ORDERED AND DECREED THAT the name of _____

_____ is hereby changed to _____.

Signed and entered this ____ day of _____, 20___.

                                    _____
                                    Judge presiding in the

                                    _____District Court

                                    _____County

                                    State of Texas

ORDER/NOTICE TO WITHHOLD INCOME FOR CHILD SUPPORT

State _____   _____ Original Order/Notice
Co./City/Dist. of _____   _____ Amended Order/Notice
Date of Order/Notice _____   _____ Terminate Order/Notice
Court/Case Number _____

_____) RE: * _____
   Employer/Withholder's Federal EIN Number) Employee/Obligor's Name (Last, First, MI)
) *
_____) _____
      Employer/Withholder's Name   ) Employee/Obligor's Social Security Number
) *
_____) _____
      Employer/Withholder's Address   ) Employee/Obligor's Case Identifier
_____)
) Custodial Parent's Name (Last, First, MI)
_____)
_____)

   Child(ren)s Name(s):   DOB   Child(ren)s Name(s):   DOB

ORDER INFORMATION: This is an Order/Notice to Withhold Income for Child Support based upon an order for support from _____.
By law, you are required to deduct these amounts from the above-named employee's/obligor's income until _____ even if the
Order/Notice is not issued by your State.

☐ If checked, you are required to enroll the child(ren) identified above in any health insurance coverage available through the employee's/obligor's employment.

$ _____ per _____ in current support
$ _____ per _____ in past-due support   Arrears 12 weeks or greater? ☐ yes ☐ no
$ _____ per _____ in medical support
$ _____ per _____ in other (specify) _____
                      per _____ in other (specify) _____
for a total of $ _____ per _____ to be forwarded to the payee below.

You do not have to vary your pay cycle to be in compliance with the support order. If your pay cycle does not match the ordered support payment cycle, use the following to determine how much to withhold:

$ _____ per weekly pay period. $ _____ per semimonthly pay period (twice a month).
$ _____ per biweekly pay period (every two weeks). $ _____ per monthly pay period.

REMITTANCE INFORMATION: Follow the laws and procedures of the employee's/obligor's principal place of employment even if such laws and procedures are different from this paragraph:

     You must begin withholding no later than the first pay period occurring _____ working days after the date of this Order/Notice. Send payment within _____ working days of the paydate/date of withholding. You are entitled to deduct a fee of _____ to defray the cost of withholding. The total withheld amount, including your fee, cannot exceed _____% of the employee/obligor's aggregate disposable weekly earnings. For the purpose of the limitation on withholding, the following information is needed (see #9 on back):

When remitting payment provide the paydate/date of withholding and the case identifier _____.
If remitting by EFT/EDI, use this FIPS code: *_____; Bank routing code: *_____;
Bank account number: *_____.

Make it payable to: _____
Send check to: _____
_____
_____
_____

Authorized by _____
Print Name   _____

ADDITIONAL INFORMATION TO EMPLOYERS AND OTHER WITHHOLDERS

☐ **If checked you are required to provide a copy of this form to your employee.**

1. **Priority:** Withholding under this Order/Notice has priority over any other legal process under State law against the same income. Federal tax levies in effect before receipt of this order have priority. If there are Federal tax levies in effect please contact the requesting agency listed below.

2. **Combining Payments:** You can combine withheld amounts from more than one employee/obligor's income in a single payment to each agency requesting withholding. You must, however, separately identify the portion of the single payment that is attributable to each employee/obligor.

3. **Reporting the Paydate/Date of Withholding:** You must report the paydate/date of withholding when sending the payment. The paydate/date of withholding is the date on which the employee is paid and controls the income, i.e. the date the income check or cash is given to the employee, or the date in which the income is deposited directly in his/her account.

4. **Employee/Obligor with Multiple Support Withholdings:** If you receive more than one Order/Notice against this employee/obligor and you are unable to honor them all in full because together they exceed the withholding limit of the State of the employee's principal place of employment (see #9 below), you must allocate the withholding based on the law of the State of the employee's principal place of employment. If you are unsure of that State's allocation law, you must honor all Orders/Notices' current support withholdings before you withhold for any arrearages, to the greatest extent possible under the withholding limit. You should immediately contact the last agency that sent you an Order/Notice to find the allocation law of the state of the employee's principal place of employment.

5. **Termination Notification:** You must promptly notify the payee when the employee/obligor no longer works for you. Please provide the information requested and return a copy of this order/notice to the agency identified below.

   EMPLOYEE'S/OBLIGOR'S NAME: _____.
   EMPLOYEE'S CASE IDENTIFIER: _____ **DATE OF SEPARATION:** _____.
   LAST KNOWN HOME ADDRESS: _____.
   NEW EMPLOYER'S ADDRESS: _____.

6. **Lump Sum Payments: You may be required to report and withhold from lump sum payments such as bonuses, commissions, or severance pay. If you have any questions about lump sum payments, contact the person or authority below.**

7. **Liability:** If you fail to withhold income as the Order/Notice directs, you are liable for both the accumulated amount you should have withheld from the employee/obligor's income and any other penalties set by State law.

8. **Anti-discrimination:** You are subject to a fine determined under State law for discharging an employee/obligor from employment, refusing to employ, or taking disciplinary action against any employee/obligor because of a child support withholding.

9. **Withholding Limits:** You may not withhold more than the lesser of: 1) the amounts allowed by the Federal Consumer Credit Protection Act (15 U.S.C. § 1673(b), or 2) the amounts allowed by the State of the employee's/obligor's principal place of employment. The Federal limit applies to the aggregate disposable weekly earnings (ADWE). ADWE is the net income left after making mandatory deductions such as: State, Federal, local taxes; Social Security taxes; and Medicare taxes. The Federal CCPA limit is 50% of the ADWE for child support and alimony, which is increased by: 1) 10% if the employee does not support a second family; and/or 2) 5% if arrears are more than 12 weeks old. (see boxes on front)

10. _____

Requesting Agency _____

If you or your employee/obligor have any questions, contact:

by telephone at _____ or
by FAX at _____ or
by Internet _____ .

Cause No._____

IN THE MATTER OF THE MARRIAGE OF:

_____ , Petitioner

AND

_____ , Respondent

IN THE DISTRICT COURT

OF _____ COUNTY

___ JUDICIAL DISTRICT

EMPLOYER'S ORDER TO WITHHOLD
EARNINGS FOR SPOUSAL MAINTENANCE

   The Court ORDERS you, the employer of PAYOR to withhold income from his/her disposable earnings from this employment as follows:

PAYOR

   Name: _____

   Address:_____

   Social Security number: _____

PAYEE

   Name: _____

   Address: _____

   Social Security number: _____

Withholding from Earnings for Spousal Maintenance

   The Court ORDERS that any employer of PAYOR shall begin withholding from his/her disposable earnings no later than the first pay period following the date this order is served on that employer.

Method of Payment

   The Court ORDERS the employer to pay all amounts withheld on each payday to PAYEE at the address stated above, or at any address provided to you by PAYEE in writing.

Order to Withhold

The Court ORDERS employer to withhold the following amounts from the earnings of PAYOR:

(1) $_____ on current spousal maintenance if PAYOR is paid monthly:

(2) $_____ on current spousal maintenance, if PAYOR is paid twice monthly:

(3) $_____ on current spousal maintenance, if PAYOR is paid every other week:

(4) $_____ on current spousal maintenance, if PAYOR is paid every week:

The Court ORDERS the employer to withhold the above amount until:

Calculating Disposable Earnings

The employer shall calculate PAYOR's disposable earnings, which are subject to withholding for child support, as follows:

1. Determine the "earnings" of PAYOR, which means compensation paid or payable for personal services, whether called wages, salary, compensation received as an independent contractor, overtime pay, severance pay, commission, bonus, or otherwise, including periodic payments pursuant to a pension, an annuity, workers' compensation, a disability and retirement program, and unemployment benefits;

2. Subtract the following sums to calculate PAYOR's "disposable earnings":
   a. any amounts required by law to be withheld, that is, federal income tax and federal FICA or OASI tax (Social Security) and Railroad Retirement Act contributions;
   b. union dues;
   c. nondiscretionary retirement contributions by PAYOR; and
   d. medical, hospitalization, and disability insurance coverage for PAYOR and payor's children.

Notice of Change of Employment

The Court ORDERS the employer to notify the Court and PAYEE within seven days of the date that PAYOR terminates employment. The Court ORDERS the employer to provide PAYOR's last known address and the name and address of his new employer, if known.

SIGNED on _____.

_____
JUDGE PRESIDING

Cause No._____

IN THE MATTER OF THE MARRIAGE OF:

_____, Petitioner

AND

                IN THE DISTRICT COURT

                OF _____ COUNTY

_____, Respondent

                ___ JUDICIAL DISTRICT

AND IN THE INTEREST OF

_____

_____ CHILD(REN)

REQUEST TO ISSUE
EMPLOYER'S ORDER TO WITHHOLD
EARNINGS FOR CHILD SUPPORT OR SPOUSAL MAINTENANCE

To the Clerk of the Court:

Please issue a certified copy of the following order(s) in this cause:
(check which order(s) should be issued)

_____ Order/Notice to Withhold from Earnings for Child Support, signed by the Court on _____ [date court signed order]

_____ Employer's Order to Withholding Earnings for Spousal Maintenance, signed by the Court on _____ [date court signed order].

And deliver the order to:

Obligor/Payor's Employer: _____

Address: _____

City, State, Zip _____

Submitted on _____.

_____
OBLIGEE/PAYEE

_____
OBLIGEE/PAYEE'S ADDRESS

Cause No._____

IN THE MATTER OF THE MARRIAGE OF:

_____, Petitioner

AND   IN THE DISTRICT COURT

_____   OF _____ COUNTY

_____, Respondent   ___ JUDICIAL DISTRICT

AND IN THE INTEREST OF

_____

_____ CHILD(REN)

FINANCIAL INFORMATION AND PROPOSED SUPPORT DECISION

    I, _____, would testify under oath in open Court that the following information is true and correct. I understand that at a Court hearing I may be required to prove these amounts by testimony and by records such as pay vouchers, cancelled checks, receipts and bills.

A. PETITIONER'S MONTHLY RESOURCES (Describe each source)	GROSS AMOUNT	ALLOWED DEDUCTIONS (Soc.Sec., union dues, w/holding tax, health insurance for child)
1. _____	$_____	$_____
2. _____	$_____	$_____
3. _____	$_____	$_____
4. _____	$_____	$_____
TOTAL RESOURCES EACH MONTH	$_____	$_____

b. RESPONDENT'S MONTHLY RESOURCES (Describe each source)	GROSS AMOUNT	ALLOWED DEDUCTIONS (Soc.Sec., union dues, w/holding tax, health insurance for child)
1. _____	$_____	$_____
2. _____	$_____	$_____
3. _____	$_____	$_____
4. _____	$_____	$_____
TOTAL RESOURCES EACH MONTH	$_____	$_____

C. TOTAL MONEY NEEDED PER MONTH BY CUSTODIAL PARENT AND MINOR CHILD(REN). (Amounts not paid monthly are averages).

1. Rent or house payment $_____   16. Clothing & shoes $_____
2. Property tax not included in item 1 $_____   17. Insurance on car $_____
  18. Insurance - Life $_____
3. Residence maintenance $_____   19. Insurance - Health $_____
4. Home insurance $_____   20. Child care $_____
5. Utilities $_____   21. Child activities $_____
6. Telephone (avge./mo.) $_____   22. Cable TV, Newspaper $_____
7. Groceries & supplies $_____   23. Other:_____ $_____
8. Meals away from home $_____   _____ $_____
9. School lunches $_____   _____ $_____
10. Dental $_____   _____ $_____
11. Medical & Medicine $_____   _____ $_____
12. Laundry, dry clean $_____   24. Support or alimony payments to others $_____
13. Gas & Car maintenance $_____
14. Entertainment $_____   25. Monthly debt payments (total of item D) $_____
15. Haircuts $_____

TOTAL NEEDED PER MONTH (Total of items C 1-25) $_____

DIFFERENCE BETWEEN MONEY RECEIVED & MONEY NEEDED $_____

D. MONTHLY PAYMENTS ON INDEBTEDNESS:

DESCRIPTION OF DEBT	BALANCE OWED	AMOUNT OF MONTHLY PMT.	DATE OF FINAL PMT.
1._____	$_____	$_____	_____
2._____	$_____	$_____	_____
3._____	$_____	$_____	_____
4._____	$_____	$_____	_____
5._____	$_____	$_____	_____
6._____	$_____	$_____	_____

TOTAL MONTHLY PAYMENTS $_____
(enter on line C 25 above)

I intend to ask the Court to set support at $_____ per month.

Signed this_____day of _____, 20___

_____, Pro Se
Petitioner

Texas Standard Schedule for the Possession of Minor Children

The next five pages contain terms that are in accord with the Texas statewide standard. They are presented in such a way that you can, if you wish, simply make the few indicated choices, tear them out and attach them to your Decree. They may seem intricate, because they try to cover all situations. If you study them carefully, it all becomes clear. Make sure you understand them very well, because these terms will affect your life for a long time to come.

Notice that the very first term gives you the freedom to live according to any schedule you like if you and your spouse can agree in advance. The rest of the terms govern what happens if your agreement should break down.

Wherever a choice is indicated in the forms, the law intends that the choice be made by the Possessory Conservator. As a practical matter, in many default situations where the Possessory Conservator is the Respondent and is not involved in discussions or won't care either way, the choices get made by the Petitioner. However, where the Possessory Conservator is actively involved or interested, he or she should be allowed to make all choices indicated.

Slight variations in these terms are allowable to suit the schedule of the parties or the child(ren), but any major departures from these terms will require either a written agreement between the parties or a clear showing of evidence that different terms are in the best interest of the child(ren).

NOTE: At item B.1 (on the next page) choose the correct title for the parents (as you stated it on page 7 of your Decree) and put their names in the appropriate blanks. Even if you have Joint Managing Conservatorship, we still use the legal shorthand "MC" and "PC" in this form to identify who is who.

SCHEDULE FOR POSSESSION OF MINOR CHILDREN

A. Mutual Agreement: The parties may have possession of the child at any and all times mutually agreed to in advance, and in the absence of mutual agreement, shall have possession of the child under the specified terms set out below.

B. General Terms and Conditions

1. The Managing Conservator _____ (hereafter MC) is ORDERED to surrender the child to the Possessory Conservator _____ (hereafter PC) at the beginning of each period of the PC's possession at the residence of the MC.

2. If the PC elects to begin a period of possession at the time the child's school is regularly dismissed, the MC is ORDERED to surrender the child to the PC at the beginning of each such period of possession at the school in which the child is enrolled.

3. The PC is hereby ORDERED to (choose one of the first two, third optional)

...surrender the child to the MC at the end of each period of possession at the residence of the PC;

...return the child to the residence of the MC at the end of each period of possession;

...If the PC's county of residence remains the same after rendition of the order establishing terms and conditions of possession and access, and if the MC's county of residence changes, effective on the date of the change of residence by the MC, the PC shall surrender the child to the MC at the end of each period of possession at the residence of the PC.

4. Each conservator is ORDERED to return with the child the personal effects that the child brought at the beginning of the period of possession.

5. Either parent may designate any competent adult to pick up and return the child, as applicable, and a parent or designated competent adult is ORDERED to be present when the child is picked up or returned.

6. A parent shall give notice to the person in possession of the child on each occasion that the parent will be unable to exercise that parent's right of possession for any specified period. Repeated failure of a parent to give notice of an inability to exercise possessory rights may be considered as a factor in a modification of those possessory rights.

7. Written notice shall be deemed to have been timely made if received or postmarked before or at the time that notice is due.

8. If a conservator's time of possession of a child ends at the time school resumes and for any reason the child will not be returned to school, the conservator in possession of the child shall immediately notify the school and the other conservator that the child will not or has not been returned to school.

9. Each party is ORDERED to give written notice of change of address to the other party, stating the intended date of change and the address of the new residence, and it shall be given at least sixty (60) days before the intended change or on the first day the party knows or should know of the change, whichever occurs first.

10. "School" means the primary or secondary school in which the child is enrolled, or if the child is not enrolled in a primary or secondary school, the public school district in which the child resides.

C. Regular Weekly Schedule

1. When the PC resides less than 100 miles from the primary residence of the child, the PC shall have the right to possession of the child as follows:
a) (choose one)
..... On weekends beginning 6 pm on the first, third and fifth Friday of each month and ending 6 pm on the following Sunday.
..... On weekends begining at the time the child's school is dismissed and ending at 6 pm on the following Sunday.
b) On Wednesdays of each week during the regular school term (choose one)
..... beginning at 6 pm and ending at 8 pm.
..... beginning at 6 pm and ending at the time the child's school resumes.
..... beginning at the time the child's school is dis-missed, ending at 8 pm
..... beginning at the time the child's school is dismissed and ending at the time the child's school resumes.

2. When the PC resides more than 100 miles from the residence of the child, the PC shall have possession of the child as follows:

a) Either regular weekend possession on the first, third and fifth Friday of each month as provided under Subsections C1 and D. However, the PC may choose an alternative schedule ONLY IF the PC gives written notice to the MC within 90 days after the parties begin to reside more than 100 miles apart. In that case the PC shall have possession as follows:

One weekend per month of the PC's choice beginning at 6 pm on the day school recesses for the weekend and ending at 6 pm on the day before school resumes after that weekend,

PROVIDED THAT the PC gives the MC seven days written or telephone notice preceding a designated weekend, and FURTHER PROVIDED THAT the weekend possession does not interfere with the vacation and holiday possession of MC in Section E below.

D. Weekends Extended by Holiday: If a weekend period of possession of the PC coincides with a school holiday during the regular school term, or with a federal, state or local holiday during the summer months when school is not in session, the weekend possession shall end at 6 pm on a Monday holiday or school holiday or shall begin at 6 pm Thursday for a Friday holiday or school holiday, as applicable.

E. Vacations and Holidays: The following periods of possession supercede any conflicting weekend or Wednesday periods of possession provided by subsections C and D above. The parents shall have rights of possession of the child as follows:

1. Christmas. The PC shall have possession of the child in even-numbered years beginning at 6 pm on the day the child is dismissed from school for the Christmas school vacation and ending at noon on December 26, and the MC shall have possession for the same period in odd-numbered years.

2. Christmas. The PC shall have possession of the child in odd-numbered years beginning at noon on December 26 and ending at 6 pm on the day before school resumes after that vacation, and the MC shall have possession for the same period in even-numbered years.

3. Thanksgiving. The PC shall have possession of the child in odd-numbered years beginning at 6 pm on the day the child is dismissed from school for Thanksgiving and ending at 6 pm on the following Sunday, and the MC shall have possession of the child for the same period in even-numbered years.

4. Spring Vacation. The PC shall have possession of the child in even-numbered years beginning at 6 pm on the day the child is dismissed from school for the school's spring vacation and ending at 6 pm on the day before school resumes after that vacation, and the MC shall have possession for the same period in odd-numbered years.

When the PC resides more than 100 miles from the residence of the child, the PC shall have possession of the child **every year** beginning at 6 pm on the day the child is dismissed from school for the school's spring vacation and ending at 6 pm on the day before school resumes after that vacation.

5. Summer Possession. If the PC:

a) gives the MC written notice by May 1 of each year specifying an extended period or periods of summer possession, the PC shall have possession of the child for 30 days beginning no earlier than the day after the child's school is dismissed for the summer vacation and ending no later than seven days prior to school resuming at the end of the summer vacation, to be exercised in no more than two separate periods of at least seven consecutive days each; or

b) does not give the MC such notice, the PC shall have possession of the child for 30 consecutive days beginning at 6 pm on July 1 and ending at 6 pm on July 31.

6. Long Distance Summer Possession. When the PC resides more than 100 miles from the residence of the child, if the PC:

a) gives the MC written notice by May 1 of each year specifying an extended period or periods of summer possession, the PC shall have possession of the child for 42 days beginning no earlier than the day after the child's school is dismissed for the summer vacation and ending no later than seven days prior to school resuming at the end of the summer vacation, to be exercised in no more than two separate periods of at least seven consecutive days each; or

b) does not give the MC such notice, the PC shall have possession of the child for 42 consecutive days beginning at 6 pm on June 15 and ending at 6 pm on July 27.

7. If the MC gives the PC written notice by June 1, the MC shall have possession of the child on any one weekend beginning Friday at 6 pm and ending Sunday at 6 pm during any one period of possession of the PC in sections 5 and 6 above, PROVIDED THAT the MC picks up the child from the PC and returns the child to that same place.

8.   a) Exemption. If the MC gives the PC written notice by May 15 of each year or gives the PC 14 days' written notice on or after May 16, the MC may designate one weekend beginning no earlier than the day after the child's school is dismissed for the summer vacation and ending no later than seven days prior to school resuming at the end of the summer vacation, during which an otherwise scheduled weekend period of possession by the PC will not take place, PROVIDED THAT the weekend does not interfere with the PC's summer possession as defined in sections 5 and 6 or with Father's Day if the PC is the father of the child.

b) Long Distance Exemption. When the PC resides more than 100 miles from the residence of the child, if the MC gives the PC written notice by June 1 of each year the MC shall have possession of the child on any one weekend beginning Friday at 6 pm and ending the following Sunday at 6 pm during any one period of possession of the PC under section 6 PROVIDED THAT the MC picks up the child from the PC and returns the child to that same place and FURTHER PROVIDED THAT if the PC shall have possession of the child for more than 30 days, the MC shall have possession on any two non-consecutive weekends.

c) MC's Designation. When the PC resides more than 100 miles from the residence of the child, if the MC gives the PC written notice by May 15 of each year or gives the PC 30 days written notice on or after May 16 of each year, the MC may designate 21 days beginning no earlier than the day after the child's school is dismissed for the summer vacation and ending no later than seven days prior to school resuming at the end of the summer vacation, to be exercised in no more than two separate periods of at least seven consecutive days each, during which the PC shall not have possession of the child, PROVIDED THAT the designated time period does not interfere with the PC's summer possession as defined in sections 5 and 6 or with Father's day if the PC is the father of the child.

9. Child's Birthday. The parent not otherwise entitled under this standard order to present possession of a child on the child's birthday shall have possession of the child beginning at 6 pm and ending at 8 pm, PROVIDED THAT, said parent pick up the child from the residence of the conservator entitled to possession and return the child to that same place.

10. Father's Day. If a conservator, the father shall have possession of the child beginning at 6 pm on the Friday preceding Father's Day and ending at 6 pm on Father's Day, provided that, if he is not otherwise entitled under this standard order to present possession of the child, he picks up the child from the residence of the conservator entitled to possession and returns the child to that same place.

11. Mother's Day. If a conservator, the mother shall have possession of the child beginning at 6 pm on the Friday preceding Mother's Day and ending at 6 pm on Mother's Day, provided that, if she is not otherwise entitled under this standard order to present possession of the child, she picks up the child from the residence of the conservator entitled to possession and returns the child to that same place.

INFORMATION ON SUIT AFFECTING THE FAMILY RELATIONSHIP
(EXCLUDING ADOPTIONS)

SECTION I   GENERAL INFORMATION (REQUIRED)   STATE FILE NUMBER

1a. COUNTY_____   1b. COURT NO. _____

1d. CAUSE NO. _____   1e. DATE OF ORDER (mm/dd/yyyy) _____

2. HAS THERE BEEN A FINDING BY THE COURT OF: ☐ DOMESTIC VIOLENCE ? ☐ CHILD ABUSE ?

3. TYPE OF ORDER (CHECK ALL THAT APPLY):

☐ DIVORCE/ ANNULMENT <u>WITH</u> CHILDREN(Sec 1, 2, 3, 4)   ☐ DIVORCE/ ANNULMENT <u>WITHOUT</u> CHILDREN(Sec 1, 2)

☐ PATERNITY <u>WITH</u> CHILD SUPPORT (Sec 1, 3, 4, 5)   ☐ PATERNITY <u>WITHOUT</u> CHILD SUPPORT (Sec 1, 3, 5)

☐ CHILD SUPPORT OBLIGATION/MODIFICATION (Sec 1, 3, 4)   ☐ TERMINATION OF RIGHTS (Sec 1, 3, 6)

☐ CONSERVATORSHIP (Sec 1, 3)   ☐ OTHER (Specify)_____

☐ TRANSFER TO (Sec 1, 3) COUNTY_____ COURT NO. _____ STATE COURT ID# _____

4a. NAME OF ATTORNEY FOR PETITIONER					4b. ATTORNEY GENERAL ACCT/CASE #
4c. CURRENT MAILING ADDRESS: STREET & NO.	CITY	STATE		ZIP	4d. TELEPHONE NUMBER ( )

SECTION 2 (IF APPLICABLE)   REPORT OF DIVORCE OR ANNULMENT OF MARRIAGE

HUSBAND	5. FIRST NAME	MIDDLE	LAST		SUFFIX	6. DATE OF BIRTH (mm/dd/yyyy)
	7. PLACE OF BIRTH CITY	STATE OR FOREIGN COUNTRY		8. RACE	9. SOCIAL SECURITY NUMBER	
	10. USUAL RESIDENCE STREET NAME & NUMBER		CITY		STATE	ZIP

WIFE	11. FIRST NAME	MIDDLE	LAST	MAIDEN	12. DATE OF BIRTH (mm/dd/yyyy)
	13. PLACE OF BIRTH CITY	STATE OR FOREIGN COUNTRY	14. RACE	15. SOCIAL SECURITY NUMBER	
	16. USUAL RESIDENCE STREET NAME & NUMBER		CITY	STATE	ZIP

17. NUMBER OF MINOR CHILDREN	18. DATE OF MARRIAGE (mmddyyyy)	19. PLACE OF MARRIAGE CITY	STATE	20. PETITIONER IS ☐ HUSBAND ☐ WIFE

SECTION 3 (IF APPLICABLE)   CHILDREN AFFECTED BY THIS SUIT

CHILD 1	21a. FIRST NAME	MIDDLE		LAST	SUFFIX	21b. DATE OF BIRTH (mm/dd/yyyy)
	21c. SOCIAL SECURITY NUMBER	21d. SEX	21e. BIRTHPLACE CITY	COUNTY		STATE
	21f. PRIOR NAME OF CHILD FIRST MIDDLE LAST SUFFIX			21g. NEW NAME OF CHILD FIRST MIDDLE LAST SUFFIX		

CHILD 2	22a. FIRST NAME	MIDDLE		LAST	SUFFIX	22b. DATE OF BIRTH (mm/dd/yyyy)
	22c. SOCIAL SECURITY NUMBER	22d. SEX	22e. BIRTHPLACE CITY	COUNTY		STATE
	22f. PRIOR NAME OF CHILD FIRST MIDDLE LAST SUFFIX			22g. NEW NAME OF CHILD FIRST MIDDLE LAST SUFFIX		

CHILD 3	23a. FIRST NAME	MIDDLE		LAST	SUFFIX	23b. DATE OF BIRTH (mm/dd/yyyy)
	23c. SOCIAL SECURITY NUMBER	23d. SEX	23e. BIRTHPLACE CITY	COUNTY		STATE
	23f. PRIOR NAME OF CHILD FIRST MIDDLE LAST SUFFIX			23g. NEW NAME OF CHILD FIRST MIDDLE LAST SUFFIX		

CHILD 4	24a. FIRST NAME	MIDDLE		LAST	SUFFIX	24b. DATE OF BIRTH (mm/dd/yyyy)
	24c. SOCIAL SECURITY NUMBER	24d. SEX	24e. BIRTHPLACE CITY	COUNTY		STATE
	24f. PRIOR NAME OF CHILD FIRST MIDDLE LAST SUFFIX			24g. NEW NAME OF CHILD FIRST MIDDLE LAST SUFFIX		

TDH
TEXAS DEPARTMENT OF HEALTH

CONTINUED ON OTHER SIDE

SECTION 4 (IF APPLICABLE)   OBLIGEE / OBLIGOR INFORMATION

OBLIGEE

THIS PARTY TO THE SUIT IS (CHECK ONE):   ☐ 25a. TDPRS   ☐ 25b. NON-PARENT CONSERVATOR - COMPLETE 26 - 32

☐ 25c. HUSBAND AS SHOWN ON FRONT OF THIS FORM - COMPLETE 31 - 32 ONLY   ☐ 25d. WIFE AS SHOWN ON FRONT OF THIS FORM - COMPLETE 31 - 32 ONLY

☐ 25e. BIOLOGICAL FATHER - COMPLETE 26 - 32   ☐ 25f. BIOLOGICAL MOTHER - COMPLETE 26 - 32

26. FIRST NAME	MIDDLE	LAST	SUFFIX	MAIDEN

27. DATE OF BIRTH (mm/dd/yyyy)	28. PLACE OF BIRTH CITY	STATE OR FOREIGN COUNTRY

29. USUAL RESIDENCE STREET NAME & NUMBER	CITY	COUNTY	STATE	ZIP

30. SOCIAL SECURITY NUMBER	31. DRIVER LICENSE NO & STATE	32. TELEPHONE NUMBER ( )

OBLIGOR #1

THIS PARTY TO THE SUIT IS (CHECK ONE):   ☐ 33a. NON-PARENT CONSERVATOR - COMPLETE 34 - 43

☐ 33b. HUSBAND AS SHOWN ON FRONT OF THIS FORM - COMPLETE 39 - 43 ONLY   ☐ 33c. WIFE AS SHOWN ON FRONT OF THIS FORM - COMPLETE 39 - 43 ONLY

☐ 33d. BIOLOGICAL FATHER - COMPLETE 34 - 43   ☐ 33e. BIOLOGICAL MOTHER - COMPLETE 34 - 43

34. FIRST NAME	MIDDLE	LAST	SUFFIX	MAIDEN

35. DATE OF BIRTH (mm/dd/yyyy)	36. PLACE OF BIRTH CITY	STATE OR FOREIGN COUNTRY

37. USUAL RESIDENCE STREET NAME & NUMBER	CITY	COUNTY	STATE	ZIP

38. SOCIAL SECURITY NUMBER	39. DRIVER LICENSE NO & STATE	40. TELEPHONE NUMBER

41. EMPLOYER NAME	42. EMPLOYER TELEPHONE NUMBER ( )

43. EMPLOYER PAYROLL ADDRESS STREET NAME & NUMBER	CITY	STATE	ZIP

OBLIGOR #2

THIS PARTY TO THE SUIT IS (CHECK ONE):   ☐ 44a. NON-PARENT CONSERVATOR - COMPLETE 45 - 54

☐ 44b. HUSBAND AS SHOWN ON FRONT OF THIS FORM - COMPLETE 50 - 54 ONLY   ☐ 44c. WIFE AS SHOWN ON FRONT OF THIS FORM - COMPLETE 50 - 54 ONLY

☐ 44d. BIOLOGICAL FATHER - COMPLETE 45 - 54   ☐ 44e. BIOLOGICAL MOTHER - COMPLETE 45 - 54

45. FIRST NAME	MIDDLE	LAST	SUFFIX	MAIDEN

46. DATE OF BIRTH (mm/dd/yyyy)	47. PLACE OF BIRTH CITY	STATE OR FOREIGN COUNTRY

48. USUAL RESIDENCE STREET NAME & NUMBER	CITY	COUNTY	STATE	ZIP

49. SOCIAL SECURITY NUMBER	50. DRIVER LICENSE NO & STATE	51. TELEPHONE NUMBER ( )

52. EMPLOYER NAME	53. EMPLOYER TELEPHONE NUMBER ( )

54. EMPLOYER PAYROLL ADDRESS STREET NAME & NUMBER	CITY	STATE	ZIP

SECTION 5 (IF APPLICABLE)   FOR ORDERS CONCERNING PATERNITY ESTABLISHMENT OF BIOLOGICAL FATHER

55. BIOLOGICAL FATHER'S NAME FIRST MIDDLE LAST SUFFIX	56. DATE OF BIRTH (mm/dd/yyyy)

57. SOCIAL SECURITY NUMBER	58. CURRENT MAILING ADDRESS STREET NAME & NUMBER CITY STATE ZIP

59. DOES THIS ORDER REMOVE INFORMATION PERTAINING TO A FATHER FROM A CHILD'S CERTIFICATE OF BIRTH? ☐ NO ☐ YES

SECTION 6   TERMINATION OF RIGHTS - Information related to the individual(s) whose rights are being terminated in this suit

60a. FIRST NAME	MIDDLE NAME	LAST NAME	SUFFIX	60b. RELATIONSHIP
61a. FIRST NAME	MIDDLE NAME	LAST NAME	SUFFIX	61b. RELATIONSHIP
62a. FIRST NAME	MIDDLE NAME	LAST NAME	SUFFIX	62b. RELATIONSHIP

Comments: _____

_____

_____

certify that the above order was granted on the
date and place as stated.

_____
SIGNATURE OF THE CLERK OF THE COURT

STATE OF TEXAS　　　　　　　)
　　　　　　　　　　　　　　　　)
COUNTY OF _____)

POWER OF ATTORNEY TO TRANSFER MOTOR VEHICLE

　　　I, _____, of the state and county named above, for good and valuable consideration constitute and appoint _____, of _____ (city, county, state) my agent and attorney in fact, in my name, place, and stead, to convey and transfer all of my right, title and interest in one _____ (year, make, model) motor vehicle, vehicle identification number _____, to whomever s/he may desire and to execute, in my name as attorney in fact, any and all instruments necessary for such conveyance and transfer.

　　　SIGNED on _____, 20___.

_____

ACKNOWLEDGEMENT

STATE OF TEXAS　　　　　　　)
　　　　　　　　　　　　　　　　)
COUNTY OF _____)

　　　This instrument was acknowledged before me on _____, 20___, by _____.

_____
Notary Public in and for the
State of Texas

How to fill out the Special Warranty Deed

A special warranty deed transfers title from one party to the other, without the party who is giving away the property guaranteeing that the chain of title is correct. If a title insurance policy was involved in the original purchase of the house and you and your spouse have not assigned away any part of your property to other parties during the marriage, you have nothing to worry about. If you purchased your house without a title policy, you may wish to contact a title company to verify that there are no "clouds" on the title, particularly if you are the person receiving the house. A title search generally costs about $100.

Do not use this deed form if you are not transferring property between spouses. It has specialized language regarding the transfer that is not applicable to a general sale of land. Consult an attorney or a title company if you have questions about other types of deeds.

Either fill in the blanks with a typewriter or retype this special warranty deed on a letter-size piece of paper. It is okay if the deed runs over to a second page.

The "Grantor" is the person giving the property and the "Grantee" is the person receiving the property.

1. Type in Grantor's name and name of county where Grantor resides.

2. Copy the cause number and style (caption) of the case as it appears on your Original Petition or Divorce Decree. If you have children you will have to add the "And in the Interest of _____ Child(ren)" block as on your other papers. That would definitely mean typing the whole warranty deed over.

   If you are filing the deed *before* you file the divorce petition, you don't need any of the court information on lines 5 to 7. Draw lines through all this starting on line 4 with "namely the division of property in:" and ending with "Judicial District Court of _____County, Texas."

3. Type in Grantee's name and name of county where Grantee resides.

4. Type the property description *exactly* as it appears on the warranty deed you received when you bought the property. It is extremely important that you list it in the same way it is spelled out, otherwise the transfer of title might be defective and cause problems later on. If you have a very long description (like a surveyor's sheet that runs for a page or more), you may want to photocopy it, attach it to the back page of the deed, and call it "Exhibit A." If so, type "See Exhibit A." in this space.

5. Skip the rest of the blanks for the moment and type in Grantee's name and address on the bottom left side of the deed.

6. The Grantor must now take the warranty deed to a Notary Public, and sign and date it in the Notary's presence. The Notary Public fills in the rest of the blank lines.

After this is all done the deed must be filed with the county clerk in the county where the property is located. There is a nominal filing fee, usually $5 for the first page and $3 for each successive page. *The deed must be filed with the county clerk in order to be valid.*

SPECIAL WARRANTY DEED

Grantor's name _____

of _____ County, Texas ("Grantor") for and in consideration of:

    The sum of TEN DOLLARS AND NO CENTS ($10.00) and other good and valuable consideration, namely the division of property in:

Cause No. _____, styled: "In the Matter of the Marriage of

_____ and _____ "

_____ Judicial District Court of _____ County, Texas

does GRANT, SELL and CONVEY to

Grantee's Name _____

of _____ County, Texas, ("Grantee"), Grantee's heirs, executors, administrators, successors or assigns, the following described real property:

Including assignments of the casualty insurance policy on the property and all escrow funds for payment of taxes and insurance premiums, to have and to hold, together with all and singular the rights and appurtenances thereto in anywise belonging forever. Grantor hereby binds Grantor, Grantor's heirs, executors, administrators, successors or assigns, to warrant and defend forever all and singular the property to Grantee, and Grantee's heirs, executors, administrators, successors or assigns against every person claiming lawfully or to claim the same or any part thereof, except as to any reservations, valid restrictions, easements, rights of way, maintenance charges, together with any lien securing the maintenance charges, zoning laws, ordinances of municipal or other governmental agencies or authorities, and conditions and covenants, if any, if applicable to and enforceable against the property described above of record when the claim is by, through or under Grantor, but not otherwise. Grantee assumes all ad valorem taxes due on the property for the current year.

    EXECUTED THIS ___ day of _____, 20___, at _____ County, Texas.

_____
GRANTOR

STATE OF TEXAS   }
COUNTY OF _____ }

    This instrument was acknowledged before me on the ___ day of _____, 20___ by _____.

_____
NOTARY PUBLIC, STATE OF TEXAS

AFTER RECORDING RETURN TO GRANTEE AT:

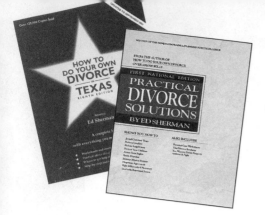

TEXAS BOOKS
&
FORMS

ORDER ONLINE AT WWW.NOLOTECH.COM
OR USE FORM BELOW, OR CALL (800) 464-5502
M-F, 9 - 5 Pacific Time

ORDER FORM

Shipping is free? Okay! Please send me:

_____ Copies of "How to Do Your Own Divorce in Texas at $19.95 ea. _____ _____

_____ Copies of "Practical Divorce Solutions" at $14.95 ea. _____ _____

FORMS SETS below are available in a paper set, or as Word and PDF files on a floppy disk. Computer forms sets can also be purchased and downloaded at **www.nolotech.com**

	Paper set	Diskette

_____ Complete sets of forms as in this book at $10.00 ea. _____ _____

_____ Forms sets for Citation by Publication or by Posting
where you have a missing/unlocatable spouse at $10.00 ea. _____ _____

_____ Both of the above sets of forms for $15 _____ _____

If ordering diskettes, indicate if for: ☐ PC ☐ Mac

Shipping and handling are free!

TOTAL ENCLOSED $ _____

Name _____

Street address _____

City, State, Zip _____

Phone _____ Fax _____ Email _____

Charge my ☐ Visa ☐ MasterCard   ☐ Check or money order is enclosed

Card number _____ Expires _____ Signed _____

MAIL THIS FORM TO: **Nolo Press Occidental**
2425 Porter Street, Suite 19
Soquel, CA 95073

Or call (800) 464-5502 to order by phone (M-F, 9 - 5 Pacific Time)